ISBN 978-1-333-90474-6
PIBN 10635167

This book is a reproduction of an important historical work. Forgotten Books uses
state-of-the-art technology to digitally reconstruct the work, preserving the original format
whilst repairing imperfections present in the aged copy. In rare cases, an imperfection in
the original, such as a blemish or missing page, may be replicated in our edition. We do,
however, repair the vast majority of imperfections successfully; any imperfections that
remain are intentionally left to preserve the state of such historical works.

1 MONTH OF
FREE
READING

at
www.ForgottenBooks.com

By purchasing this book you are eligible for one month membership to ForgottenBooks.com, giving you unlimited access to our entire collection of over 1,000,000 titles via our web site and mobile apps.

To claim your free month visit:
www.forgottenbooks.com/free635167

LEVANT INTERPRETER;

POLÝGLOT DIALOGUE BOOK

FOR

ENGLISH TRAVELLERS IN THE LEVANT.

BY

REV. ANTON TIEN, Ph.D., M.R.A.S.,

FORMERLY FIRST-CLASS INTERPRETER TO THE ALLIED FORCES IN THE CRIMEA.

WILLIAMS AND NORGATE,

14, HENRIETTA STREET, COVENT GARDEN, LONDON;
AND 20, SOUTH FREDERICK STREET, EDINBURGH.

1879.

HERTFORD:

PRINTED BY STEPHEN AUSTIN AND SONS.

PREFACE.

THE LEVANT has always been celebrated for beauty, interest, and mercantile pursuits.

At the present time it possesses a double interest for Englishmen, owing to the cession of Cyprus and the Protectorate of Asia Minor, which will bring this country in closer contact with Turkey than heretofore.

Owing to the number of nationalities dwelling in the Levant, language there is necessarily cosmopolitan; and as English travellers are seldom conversant with Oriental tongues, this Interpreter is offered to them. Very simple but useful phrases are arranged; and to facilitate the use of the little book, in compliance with the valued suggestion of my friend, W. S. W. VAUX, Esq., Secretary of the Royal Asiatic Society, the work has been rendered entirely in Roman letters.

The Greek is the modern language in common use, which differs somewhat from the old Hellenic.

The Turkish is arranged according to the system of orthography by Mr. Redhouse; the pronunciation of both being similar to that of the Italian.

With this in view, a little practice will enable any one to read with tolerable accuracy in the three Levantine languages which are spoken generally throughout the Ottoman Empire.

CONTENTS.

CONTENTS.

CONTENTS.

CONTENTS.

ERRATA.

PAGE.	LINE.	FOR.	READ.
3	3	eglio	egli
23	12	ordinatioi	ordinali
26	18	idèhim	idèyim.
28	36	yānishdasin	yāghnishdasin
30	31	ghèdègagim	ghèdèjaghim
30	32	ayrilāgiāgiz	ayrilājiāghiz
31	7	parto	parlo
31	12	lene	bene
32	4	ghègjaniz	ghèjaniz
40	11	dàka	dàba
40	25	ùmīdr	ùmīd
40	26	òluzissa	òlurissa
43	28	faginoli	fagiuoli
45	16	magiate	mangiate
45	17	magiato	mangiato
50	15	dògnuz	dònguz
56	6	dushegadir	dushejakdir
56	10	ghalayur	ghaliyur
57	9	siama	siamo
60	15	yèngidan	yènghidan
62	15	òlmogha	òlmagha
67	18	tree	tre
73	8	vederbi	vedervi
77	10	fiori	fiore
80	11	khàli	khàyli
80	13	ìshsān	ihsān
81	15	scheglietevi	sceglietevi
100	20	sày	sòy
102	2	ùhinda	ùlènda
104	14	dùshùmayasiniz	dùshùnmayasiniz.
105	7	servita	servito
111	21	sone	sono
116	11	mùzhdé	mù"àhedé
126	10	bìz	bìr
126	19	kàrkmaniz	kòrkmaniz
127	10	arrivaremo	arriveremo
128	12	ghèlejami	ghèlèjakmi
128	13	ghìdajadir	ghìdajakdir
135	16	sofririò	sofrirò
136	9	ìahta	ishta
142	1	nà"lbanda	nà"lbana

In p. 14, line 5, omit the word " dexterous "

THE

LEVANT INTERPRETER.

ENGLISH. TURKISH.

Chapter I.

Personal Pronouns.	*Zàmīr.*
I.	bèn.
Thou.	sèn.
He.	ò.
We.	biz.
Ye, you.	siz.
They.	ónlar.

AUXILIARY VERBS.

Present.	*Fi"ller.*
I am.	īm.
Thou art.	sèn.
He is.	dir.
We are.	īz.
You are.	sīniz.
They are.	dirler.

Imperfect.

I was.	ìdim *or* òlùrdim.
Thou wast.	ìdin *or* òlùrdin.
He was.	ìdi *or* òlùrdi.
We were.	ìdik *or* òlùrdik.
You were.	ìdiniz *or* òlùrdiniz.
They were.	ìdiler *or* òlùrdiler.

Perfect.

I have been.	òldim.
Thou hast been.	òldin.
He has been.	òldi.
We have been.	òldik.
Ye *or* you have been.	òldiniz.
They have been.	òldiler.

Future.

I shall *or* will be.	òlajaghim.
Thou wilt be.	òlajaksin.
He will be.	òlajak.

ITALIAN.   GREEK.

Pronomi.

Io.	eghó.
tu.	esi.
eglio.	ekino.
noi.	emees. mas. emas.
voi.	sees. esees. sas.
eglino.	ekini.

Il verbo " essere."

Presente.   *To rima.*

io sono.	eeme.
tu sei.	eese.
egli é.	eene.
noi siamo.	eemetha.
voi siete.	eesthe.
eglino sono.	eene.

Imperfetto.

io era.	imoon *or* imin.
tu eri.	isoon, iso.
egli era.	ito.
noi eravamo.	imetha.
voi eravate.	isthe *or* isasthe.
eglino erano.	isan *or* iton.

Perfetto.

io fui.	imin.
tu fosti.	iso.
egli fu.	ito.
noi fummo.	imetha.
voi foste.	isthe.
eglino furono.	isan.

Futuro.

io saró.	tha eeme.
tu sarai.	tha eese.
egli sará.	tha eene.

ENGLISH.	TURKISH.
We shall *or* will be.	òlajaghiz.
You will be.	òlajaksiniz.
They will be.	òlajakler.

Imperative.

Be thou.	òl.
Let him be.	òlsun.
Let us be.	òlalim.
	òliniz.
Let them be.	òlsunler.

Infinitive Participle.

To be. Being. Been.	òlmak. òlub. òlmish im.

The Verb "To Have." "vàr."

Present.

I have.	bènim vàr.
Thou hast.	sènin vàr.
He has.	ònūn vàr.
We have.	bìzim vàr
You have.	sìzin vàr.
They have.	ònlarin vàr.

Imperfect.

I had.	bènim vàr idi.
Thou hadst.	sènin vàr idi.
He had.	ònūn vàr idi.
We had.	bìzim vàr idi.
You had.	sìzin vàr idi.
They had.	ònlarin vàr idi.

Perfect.

I had *or* have had.	bènim vàr idi.
Thou hadst *or* hast had.	sènin vàr idi.
He had *or* has had.	ònūn vàr idi.
We had *or* have had.	bìzim vàr idi.
You had *or* have had.	sízin vàr idi.
They had *or* have had.	ònlarin vàr idi.

Future.

I shall *or* will have.	bènim òlur.
Thou shalt *or* wilt have.	sènin òlur.

ITALIAN.	GREEK.
noi saremo.	tha eemetha.
voi sarete.	tha eesthe.
eglino saranno.	tha eene.

Imperativo.

sia tu.	as eese.
sia egli.	as eene.
siamo noi.	as eemesten.
siate voi.	as ceste.
siano eglino.	as eene.

Infinitivo Participio.

essere, essendo, essuto.	ceme. eene. ceso.

Il verbo " avere."	To rima " Ekho."

Presente.

io ho.	ekho.
tu hai.	ekhees.
egli ha.	ekhee.
noi abbiamo.	ekhomen.
voi avete.	ekhete.
eglino hanno.	ekhoosin, ekhoon.

Imperfetto.

io aveva.	eekha.
tu ayevi.	eekhes.
egli aveva.	eekhe.
noi avevamo.	eekhamen.
voi avevate.	eekhete.
eglino avevano.	eekhan.

Preterito.

io ebbi.	eekha.
tu avesti.	eekhes.
egli ebbe.	eekhe.
noi avemmo.	eekhamen.
voi aveste.	eekhete.
eglino ebbero.	eekhan.

Futuro.

io avró.	tha ekho.
tu avrai.	tha ekhis.

ENGLISH.	TURKISH.
He shall *or* will have.	ònūn òlur.
We shall *or* will be.	bìzin òlur.
You shall *or* will be.	sízin òlur.
They shall *or* will be.	ònlarin òlur.

Imperative.

Hast thou.	òl sèn.
Let him have.	òlsun ò.
Let us have.	òlalim bíz.
	òlaniz síz.
Let them have.	òlsunler ònlar.

Infinitive Participles.

To have.　Having.　Had.	òlmak, bènim vàr iken,
	bènim vàr idi.

CHAPTER II.

VOCABULARY.	MUKHTASSAR-LUGHAT-KITABI.
Give me.	vèr bāna.
Some bread.	bir-āz èkmek.
Some meat.	bir-āz èt.
Some wine.	bir-āz shàrāb (shàrap).
Some fruit.	bir-āz yèmish.
Some apples.	èlma.
A pear.	bir àrmud.
A peach.	bir shèftali.
Some cherries.	bir-āz kiraz.
Some plums.	bir-āz èrik.
Some grapes.	bir-āz ùzum.
Some almonds.	bir-āz bàdem.
Some raspberries.	bir-āz izmàwla.
An orange.	bir pòrtakàl.
Some strawberries.	bir-āz chileyk.
An apricot.	bir kàyssi (zèrdāli).
A fig.	bir injiir.
Some walnuts.	bir-āz jèviz.
Some nuts.	bir-az fìndik.
Some currants.	bir-āz firènk ùzumu.

ITALIAN.	GREEK.
egli avrá.	tha ekhi.
noi avremo.	tha ekhomen.
voi avrete.	tha ekhete.
eglino avranno.	tha ekhoon.

Imperativo.

abbi tu.	ekhi esi.
abbia egli.	ekhi ekino.
abbiamo noi.	ekhomen emees.
abbiate voi.	ekhete sees, sas.
abbiano eglino.	ekhoon ekini.

Infinitivo Participio.

avere.   avendo, avuto.   ekho. on. oosa. on.

VOCABOLARIO. ONOMASTIKON.

datemi	doté mi.
del pane.	arton, psomi.
della carne.	kreas.
del vino.	enoo, krassi.
delle frutta.	oporika.
delle pome, mele.	mèla.
una pera.	en apidion.
una pesca.	en rodakinon.
delle ciriegie.	kerasia.
delle susine.	damaskina.
dell' uva.	stafilia.
delle mandorle.	amigdala.
dei lamponi.	smeoora.
una orangia.	en portogalion.
delle fragole.	fragoles.
un' albicocca.	en perikokon.
un fico.	en ziken.
delle noci.	karidia.
delle nocciuole.	leftookaria, foontookia.
del ribes.	ribissia.

ENGLISH.	TURKISH.
A chestnut.	bir kèsstānè.
A lemon.	bir lūmòn.
Some beef.	bir-āz sighir-èti.
Some mutton.	bir-āz kòyun-èti.
Some veal.	bir-āz dàna-èti.
Some ham.	bir-āz bùt (kàynàk).
Some roast meat.	bir-āz kèbàb-èti.
Some boiled beef.	bir-āz sùyush sighir-èti.
Bring me	ghetir bāna.
Some meat pie.	bir-āz tèbèvvul-et.
Some butter.	bir-āz tèrè-yagh.
Some cheese.	bir-āz pēnir.
Some eggs.	yìmurta.
Some milk.	bir-āz sùt.
Some coffee.	bir-āz kàhwé.
Some tea.	bir-āz chày.
Some cream.	bir-āz kàymak.
A cake.	bir-āz kùrābìyyé.
Some salad.	bir-āz sàlata.
Some salt.	bir-āz tūz.
Some pepper.	bir-āz bìber.
Some vinegar.	bir-āz sìrkè.
Some oil.	bir-āz zeìtūn yàgh.
Some mustard.	bir-āz khàrdàl.
Some sugar.	bir-āz shèker.
Some spices.	bir-āz bàhār.
A knife.	blehak.
A fork.	chàtal.
A spoon.	kāshìk.
A glass.	kādeh.
A serviette.	fūta.
A table-cloth.	sòfra-bèzi.
A plate.	tàbāk.
A dish.	sahn.
A basin.	kyāssé.
A bottle.	shìshè.
Some gold.	bir-āz āltin.
Some silver.	ghyùmush.
Some iron.	bir-āz tīmūr.
Some steel.	bir-āz chèlik.
Some copper.	bir-āz bākir.

ITALIAN.	GREEK.
una castagna.	en kastanon.
un limone.	en lemonion.
del manzo.	bodinon.
del castrato.	tragion kreas.
del vitello.	moskarision kreas.
del prosciuto.	khiromerion.
dell' arrosto.	psiton.
del lesso.	braston.
Portatemi	férété mi.
del pasticcio.	pastitzion.
del butirro.	bootiron.
del formagio.	tīron.
delle uove.	avga.
del latte.	ghala.
del caffé.	kafen.
del te.	tīon.
della crema.	afrogala.
una foccacia.	mīa pittan.
dell' insalata.	tsalatan.
del sale.	ālas.
del pepe.	piperion.
dell' aceto.	oksos (ksidi).
dell' olio.	eleon (ladi).
della moztarda.	zinapion.
dello zucchero.	zakharin.
degli aromi.	aromata.
un coltello.	en makherion.
una forchetta.	en pīronnion.
un cucchiajo.	en khooliarion.
un bicchiere.	en potirion.
un tovagliolo.	en khīronaktron (petzetta).
un tovaglia.	en trapezomantilon.
un tondo.	en pinakion.
un piatto.	mīa ablada.
un tazzone.	en lekanion.
una bottiglia.	mīa fialin.
dell' oro.	khrisos.
dell' argento.	arghiros (asimion).
del' ferro.	zideros.
dell' acciajo.	ksàlips.
del rame.	ksàlkos.

ENGLISH.	TURKISH.
Some brass.	bir-āz pirinj.
Some lead.	bir-āz kùrshun.
Some pewter.	bir-āz bèyāz-mà''den.
Tin.	bir-āz tènéké.
Paper.	kyāghid.
Some pens.	kālem.
A pen-knife.	kālemtrāsh.
A book.	kìtāb.
Some ink.	bir-āz mùrèkkèb.
A house.	èv.
A room.	òda.
A villa.	yāli.
A garden.	bāghcha.
A wall.	dīwàr.
Some flowers.	bir-āz chichek.
Some trees.	āghaj.

CHAPTER III.

VOCABULARY (*continued*).

A coat.	sètri.
A waistcoat.	yèlek.
A jacket.	mìntàn.
Stockings.	chòrap.
Shoes.	kùndura.
A hat.	shàpka.
A shirt.	ghyùmlek.
Linen.	chàmàshir.
A handkerchief.	mèndil.
Gloves.	èldivèn.
A comb.	tàrak.
A watch.	sā''at.
A snuff box.	ènfìyyé-kùtussu.
A table.	sòfra.
A chair.	sàndāliyyé.
A shawl.	shàl.
An arm chair.	kòltuklu.
A bed.	yàtak.
A pin.	tòplu.

ITALIAN.	GREEK.
dell' ottone.	orīkhalko.
del piombo.	mòlibdos.
dello stagno.	kossiteros (kalei).
della latta.	tenekes.
della carta.	khartion.
delle penne.	kondilia.
un temperino.	kondilomakheron.
un libro.	en biblion.
dell' inchiostro.	melane.
una casa.	mia īkia (spiti).
una camera.	en demation.
un casino.	en agrokipion.
un giardino.	en peribolion.
un muro.	toīkhos.
dei fiori.	ànthi.
degli alberi.	dendra.

Capitolo III.

un abito.	en forema.
un gilè.	ghelekon.
una vesta.	mīa besta.
delle calze.	peripodia (tsorapia).
delle scarpe.	embades (papootsia).
un capello.	pīlos (kapellon).
una camicia	īpokamison.
della biancheria.	astrorookha.
un fazzoletto.	rinomaktron (mantilion).
dei guanti.	khiroktia.
un pettine	ktenion.
un orilogio	òròlogion.
una tabacchiera.	tampakothiki.
una tavola.	trapetsa.
una sedia (seggiola).	edra.
uno sciallo.	tsialion.
una seggiola a braccio.	polithrona.
un letto.	klini.
una spilla.	karfizza.

ENGLISH.	TURKISH.
A cap.	fèss.
A purse.	kèyssé.
Spectacles.	ghyùzluk.
A razor.	ùsstura.
A dress.	rūba.
Silk.	ìpèk.
Cotton.	pāmbuk.
Thread.	ìplik.
A needle.	ìghné.
A thimble.	yùksuk.
Scissors.	màkass.
Some ribbon.	shìrit.
A horse.	āt.
A dog.	kyùpék.
A monkey.	màymūn.
A cat.	kèdi.
A mare.	kìssràk.
A cow.	īnek.
A goat.	kèchi.
A parlour.	sèlāmlik-òdassi.
A reward.	mùkyāfāt.
Pleasure.	kèyf.
Gratitude.	shùkr.
A fever.	sitma.
Some powder.	tòz *or* bir-āz bàrut.
Fine weather.	ghyùzèl-hàwā.
Some rain.	yàghmur.
A carpet.	kālī (hàli).
A boat.	kàyik.
A holiday.	tà"tīl.
A concert.	chàlghi-mèjlissi.
An illness.	khàsstalik.
A bird.	kùsh.
An appetite.	ìshtihā.
The courage.	jèssārèt.
Grief.	kìder, kàssāvet, dèrd.
The misfortune.	kàzā, bèlā.
The boldness.	jèshūrèt.
Relations.	khìssm, àkrabā.
The happiness.	sà"ādèt.
A friend.	dòsst.

ITALIAN.	GREEK.
una berreta.	skonfia.
una borsa.	tsakkoola.
degli occhiali.	òmmatooalia.
un razojo.	ksirofion.
una veste.	en forema.
della seta.	metaksion.
del cotone.	bambakion.
del filo.	klosti.
un ago.	belona, belonion.
un ditale.	daktilithra.
delle forbici.	psalidion.
della fettuccia.	tenia (kordella).
un cavallo.	īs eppes (en alegon).
un cane.	īs kion (skiles).
una scimia.	īs pithikos.
un gatto.	mīa ghata.
una cavalla.	mīa forada.
una vacca.	mīa aghelada.
una capra.	mīa ghida.
una sala.	mīa ethoosa.
un recompenso.	mīa antamibi.
del piacere.	ideni, evkharistisis.
della gratitudine.	evgnomosini.
una febre.	piretos (thermi).
della polvere.	kenis (skoni).
bel tempo.	kalos kheros.
della pioggia.	brokhi.
un tapette.	tapis.
una barca.	pliarion.
vacanza, concerto.	edīa.
un concerto.	moosiki simfonia.
una malattia.	àsthenia, arrostīa.
un uccello.	en ptinon, poolion.
dell' appetito.	orexis.
il corraggio.	i andria, to tharros.
del dolore.	ausareskīa, anīa.
la sventura.	i distikhīa.
l'ardire.	i tolmi.
dei parenti.	zinngenīs.
la felicità.	i evtikhīa.
un amico.	īs filos.

ENGLISH.	TURKISH.
Very glad.	chòk mèmnūn.
Idle.	bòsh, ishsiz.
Inquisitive.	mèrākli.
Generous.	sàkhāvetli.
Dexterous.	
Happy.	sà''īd, mèssūr.
Unhappy.	dèrdli.
Busy.	mèshghūl.
Tired.	yòrghun.
In bed, lying down.	yàtakda.
Shut.	kàpali.
Poor.	fàkīr.
Obedient.	mūtī''.
Sorry, angry.	mūté'èssif, dàrghin.
Surprised.	tà''àjjub.
Quiet.	sùss, ùsslu.
Wounded.	yàralu.
Greedy.	àch-ghyùzlu.
Ready.	hāzir.
Learned.	''ālim.
Hump-backed.	kàmpur.
Glad, merry.	mémnūn, fèrāh.
Rich.	zènghin.
Weak.	zà''īf.
Rash.	hìzli-àkish.
Imprudent.	àklsiz, dèli.
Useless.	fā'idèssiz.
Barbarous.	kàba, tòrbìyyéssiz.
Guilty.	kàbāhatli.
Wicked.	ghyùnāh, fèna.
Honest.	dòghru, èhli-''irz.
Polite.	chélébi, tèrbiyyéli.
Just.	''adil.
Wise.	''ākil.
Faithful.	sādik.
Strong.	kùvvètli.
Innocent.	kàbāhatsiz.
Dumb.	dìlsiz.
Skilful.	hùnerli.
Tame.	àlishmish.
Tall.	ùzun-boylu.

ITALIAN.	GREEK.
contentissimo.	evthimos, khiron.
pigro.	okniros.
curioso.	periergos.
generoso.	megalopsikhos.
felice.	evtikhos.
infelice.	atikhis.
occupato.	apiskholimenos.
stanco.	koorosmenos.
coricato.	plagiasmenos.
chiuso.	klīsmenos.
povero.	plokhos.
obbediente.	ipikhoos, evpīthis.
dispiaciuto, rabiato.	kakiomenos.
sorpreso.	ekpepligmenos.
tranquillo, quieto.	isikhos.
ferito.	pligomenos.
avido.	pleonektis.
pronto.	prothimos.
dotto.	logios.
gobbo.	kirtos.
allegro.	kheron.
ricco.	ploosios.
debole.	adinatos.
temerario.	tolmiros.
imprudente.	aperiskeptos.
inutile	anofelis.
barbaro.	barbaros, skliros.
colbevole.	enokhos, axiopinos.
cattivo.	kakos.
onesto.	timios.
gentile.	politicos, evgenekos.
giusto.	dikeos.
saggio.	sofos, fronimos.
fedele.	pistos.
forte.	iskhiros.
innocente.	athoōs, aploos.
muto.	bobos.
abile.	epitīthīos.
docile.	imeros.
lungho.	megas.

ENGLISH.	TURKISH.
Short, small.	kìssa.
Equal.	mùssāvi.
Bold.	jèssūr.
Proud.	kìbīrli.
Blind.	kyùr.
Young.	ghènj.
Deaf.	sàghir.
Diligent.	chàlishkhàn.
Blue.	māvi.
Merry.	shèn, fèrāh.
Dull.	issti"dādsiz.
Studious.	òkùmush.
Discreet.	"ākelli.
Ungrateful.	nānkyūr.
Ashamed.	màhjūb.
Ill.	zārar.
Wet.	yàsh.
Astonished.	tà"àjjub.
Worthy.	dègherli.
Illustrious.	mèshhūr.
Obstinate.	"ìnādji.
Modest.	màhjūb.
Excusable.	"ùzrli.
Lavish.	mùssrif.
Lame.	tòpàl.
Lucky.	bàkhtli.
Full.	dòlu.
Impolite.	tèrbiyyésiz.
Frank.	dòghru.
Narrow.	dàr.
Satisfied, pleased.	rìzālu, mùnāssib-ghyùrmek.
Displeased.	ghyùjuna-ghitmek.
Wide.	ènli.
Amiable.	ghyùzèl-ghùylu.
Ridiculous.	màsskharalik.
Heavy.	àghir.

Verbs, "To love," "To like."   "sèvmek."

To forsake.	bràkmak.
To bark.	hàwlamak.
To finish.	bìtmek.

ITALIAN.	GREEK.
piccolo.	mikros.
eguale.	isos.
ardito.	tolmiros.
orgoglioso.	iperifanos.
cieco.	tiflos.
giovane.	neos.
sordo.	kofos.
diligente.	takhis.
azzurro.	galazios.
allegro.	evfrosinos, fedros.
tristro.	avtimenos, penthimos.
studioso.	epimelis īs tin spoodin.
discreto.	fronimos.
ingrato.	akharistos.
vergognoso.	entropalos.
malato.	asthenis.
bagnato.	igros.
maravigliato.	aporon, ekthampos.
degno.	aksios.
illustre.	perifimos.
ostinato.	idiognomos.
modesto.	metriofron.
scusabile.	zingnostos, aksios.
podigo	asotos.
zoppo.	estreblomenos, anapiros.
fortunato.	evtikhis.
pieno.	pliris, ghematos.
scortese.	apolitevtos.
schietto.	īlikrinis.
stretto.	stenos.
contento.	evkhoristèmenos.
malcontento.	disarestimenos.
largo.	platis.
amabile.	aksiaghabitos.
ridicolo.	ghelios.
pesante.	baris, enokhlitikos.

"amare, piacere."

"aghapo."

abbandonare.	afino.
abbaiare.	ghavghizo.
finire.	teliono.

ENGLISH.	TURKISH.
To buy.	sàtin-àlmak.
To call.	chāghirmak.
To bring.	ghètirmak.
To light.	yàkmak.
To pull, to pluck.	chèkmek.
To tie.	bàghlamak.
To dress.	ghímek.
To assure.	tè'mīn-ètmek.
To confess.	ìkràr-ètmek.
To christen.	wàftiz-ètmek.
To sweep.	sùpurmek.
To blame.	kàbabāt-bùlmak.
To hurt.	àjitmek.
To stop.	dùrmak.
To embroider.	īné-ìshi-ètmek.
To grind.	ùghutmek.
To burn.	yànmak.
To brush.	sùpurmek.
To bridle.	gbèm-wùrmak.
To break.	**kìrmak.**
To hide.	sàklanmak.
To change.	dìghishmek.
To load.	yùklètmek.
To warm.	ìssitmak.
To seal.	mùhurlémek.
To look for.	àramak.
To chastise.	tèrbìyyé-vérmek.
To begin.	bàshlamak.
To sing.	tùrku-chàghirmak.
To cut.	kèssmek.
To tear.	yìrtmak.
To guess.	tàkhmīn-ètmek.
To make haste.	chàbik-òlmak.
To breakfast.	kàhwàlti-etmek.
To listen to.	dìnglémek (dīnémek).
To borrow.	ùdunj-àlmak.
To study.	òkumak.
To strike.	**wùrmak.**
To fry.	kàwurmak.
To rub.	sùrmek.
To spoil.	bòzmak.
To throw away.	àtmak.

ITALIAN.	GREEK.
comprare.	aghoraso.
chiamare.	kraso.
portare.	fero, kanbale.
accendere.	anapto.
strappare.	apospo.
legare.	sisfingho, prosarto.
vestire.	etimaso.
assicurare.	bebeono.
confessare.	omologho.
battezzare.	baptiso.
scopare.	kathariso, sarono.
bissimare.	elengxo, memfome.
ferire.	plighono.
fermare.	stooppono.
ricamare.	kento.
macinare.	katasintribo.
bruciare.	katakeo.
spazzare.	boortsizo.
imbrigliare.	khalinono.
rompere.	sinthraō.
nascondere.	kripto.
cambiare.	allazo.
caricare.	ferteno.
scaldare.	thermeno, zesteno.
sigillare.	boollono.
cercare.	zito.
castigare.	timoro.
cominciare.	arkhiso.
cantare.	traghondo, ado.
tagliare.	kopte, temno.
stracciare.	skhiso.
indovinare.	profitevo, manteve.
fare presto.	spevdo, spondaso.
fare colazione.	proghevome.
ascoltare.	akono.
prestare.	danīsome.
studiare.	meleto.
battere.	ktipo.
friggere.	tino, feno.
fregare.	tribo.
guastare.	khalo, fthīso.
gettare.	ripto.

CHAPTER IV.

CARDINAL NUMBERS.

ENGLISH.	TURKISH.
One.	bìr.
Two.	ìki.
Three.	ùch.
Four.	dùrt.
Five.	bèsh.
Six.	àlti.
Seven.	yèdi.
Eight.	sèkiz.
Nine.	dòkuz.
Ten.	òn.
Eleven.	òn bìr.
Twelve.	òn ìki.
Thirteen.	òn ùch.
Fourteen.	òn dùrt.
Fifteen.	òn bésh.
Sixteen.	òn àlti.
Seventeen.	òn yèdi.
Eighteen.	òn sèkiz.
Nineteen.	òn dòkuz.
Twenty.	yìghirmi.
Twenty-one.	yìghirmi bìr.
Twenty-two.	yìghirmi ìki.
Twenty-three.	yìghirmi ùch.
Twenty-four.	yìghirmi dùrt.
Twenty-five.	yìghirmi bèsh.
Twenty-six.	yìghirmi àlti.
Twenty-seven.	yìghirmi yèdi.
Twenty-eight.	yìghirmi sèkiz.
Twenty-nine.	yìghirmi dòkuz.
Thirty.	òtuz.
Thirty-one, etc.	òtuz bìr.
Forty.	kirk.
Forty-one, etc.	kirk bìr.
Fifty.	èlli.
Sixty.	àltmish.
Seventy.	yètmish.
Eighty.	sèksèn.

ITALIAN.	GREEK.
uno.	mīa, ena.
due.	dīo.
tre.	trīa.
quattro.	tessara.
cinque.	pente.
sei.	eks.
sette.	eptá.
otto.	októ.
nove.	ennea.
dieci.	deka.
undici.	endéka.
dodici.	dodèka.
tredici.	dekatrīa.
quattordici.	dekatessara.
quindici.	dekapente.
sedici.	dekaeks.
diecisette.	dekaeptá.
dieciotto.	dekaoktó.
diocinove.	dekaennea.
venti.	íkosi.
ventuno.	íkosi ena.
ventidue.	íkosi dīo.
ventitre.	íkosi trīa.
ventiquattro.	íkosi tessara.
venticinque.	íkosi pente.
ventisei.	íkosi eks.
ventisette.	íkosi eptà.
ventiotto.	íkosi októ.
ventinove.	íkosi ennea.
trenta.	trīakonta (trīanta).
trentuno, etc.	trīakonta ena, etc.
quaranta.	tessarakonta (saranta).
quarantuno, etc.	tessarakonta ena.
cinquanta.	peninta.
sessanta.	eksinta.
settanta.	ebdominta.
ottanta.	oghdonta.

ENGLISH.	TURKISH.
Ninety.	dòksàn.
A hundred.	yùz.
Hundred and one, etc.	yùz bìr.
Hundred and two, etc.	yùz ìki.
Two hundred.	ìkiyùz.
Three hundred.	ùchyùz.
A thousand.	bìng.
Two thousand.	ìki-bing.
Ten thousand.	òn bing.
A hundred thousand.	yùz bing.
A million, one million.	bìr million.

ORDINAL NUMBERS.

First.	bìrinji.
Second.	ìkinji.
Third.	ùchingi.
Fourth.	dùrtinji.
Fifth.	bèshinji.
Sixth.	àltinji.
Seventh.	yèdinji.
Eighth.	sèkizinji.
Ninth.	dòkuzinji.
Tenth.	òninji.
Eleventh.	òn bìrinji.
Twelfth.	òn ìkinji.
Twentieth	yìghirminji.
Twenty-first	yìghirmi bìrinji.
Thirtieth	òtuzinji.
Fortieth	kirkinji.
Fiftieth	ellinji.
Sixtieth	àltmishinji.
Seventieth.	yètmishinji.
Eightieth.	sèksaninji.
Ninetieth.	dòkuzaninji.
Hundredth.	yùzinji.
Hundred and first.	yùz birinji.
Hundred and second.	yùz ìkinji.
Two hundredth.	ìkiyùzinji.
Thousandth.	bíninji.
Millionth.	millioninji.

ITALIAN.	GREEK.
novanta.	eneninta.
cento.	ekaton.
centuno, etc.	ckaton ena.
centodue, etc.	ekaton dīo.
duecento.	diakosīa.
trecento.	trīakosīa.
mille.	khīlia.
due mille.	dīo khīliades.
dieci mille.	deka khīliades.
cento mila.	ekaton khīliades.
un milione.	ekatommirion.

NUMERI ORDINATIOI.　　TAKTIKA ARITHMITIKA.

primo.	protos.
secondo.	devteros.
terzo.	tritos.
quarto.	tetartos.
quinto.	pemptos.
sesto.	ektos.
settimo.	ebdomos.
ottavo.	oghdoos.
nono.	ennatos.
decimo.	dekatos.
undecimo.	endekatos.
duodecimo.	dodekatos.
ventesimo.	eēkostos.
ventesimo primo.	eekostos protos.
trentesimo.	trīakostos.
quarantesimo.	tesserakostos.
cinquantesimo.	penticostos.
sessantesimo.	etekostos.
settantesimo.	ebdomikostos.
ottantesimo.	oghdoikostos.
novantesimo.	enenikostos.
centesimo.	ekatostos.
centesimo primo.	ekatostos protes.
centesimo secondo.	ekatostos devteros.
duecentesimo.	dīakoseostos.
millesimo.	kheleostostos.
milionesimo.	ekatommereostos.

ENGLISH.	TURKISH.

FRACTIONS. KISSM.

Half.	yàrim.
Third.	ùchunju.
Quarter, fourth.	chèyrek, rùb".

MULTIPLE NUMBERS. TUREYISH, ZARB

| Double, twofold. | iki-kàt. |
| Treble, threefold. | ùch-kàt. |

THE SEASONS. MEVSIMLER.

Spring.	bàhār.
Summer.	yàz.
Autumn.	ghyùz, sòng-bàhār.
Winter.	kìsh..

THE MONTHS. AYLER.

January.	kyānūni-sānī.
February.	shùbàt.
March.	màrt.
April.	nīssān.
May.	māyiss.
June.	hàzīrān.
July.	tèmmūz.
August.	àghosstoss.
September.	èylūl.
October.	tèshrīni-èvvel.
November.	tèshrīni-sānī.
December.	kyānūni-èvvel.

THE DAYS OF THE WEEK. HAFTANIN GHYUNLERI.

Sunday.	pàzār-ghyùnu.
Monday.	pàzār-èrtéssi.
Tuesday.	sàli.
Wednesday.	chìhàrshènbèh.
Thursday.	pèrshambèh.
Friday.	jùm"à.
Saturday.	jùm"à-èrtéssi.

HOLIDAYS. TA"TIL, YORTU.

| New Year's Day. | yīl-bàshi. |
| Epiphany. | è"ssanin mèvlud ghyùni. |

ITALIAN.	GREEK.
FRAZIONI.	**KLASMATA.**
metà.	enese (meson).
la terza parte.	en treton.
la quarta parte.	en tetarton.
NUMERI MOLTIPLICI.	**POLLA PLASEASTEKA.**
doppio.	deploon.
triplo.	treploon.
LE STAGIONI.	**EE KAREE TOO ENEAVTOO.**
la primavera.	to ear.
l'estate.	to theros.
l'autunno.	to ftheuoporon.
l'inverno.	o kheeruon.
I MESI.	**EE MEENAS.**
gennajo.	yanooareos.
febbrajo.	febrooareos.
marzo.	marteos.
aprile.	apreleos.
maggio.	maeeos.
giugno.	yooneos.
luglio.	yooleos.
agosto.	aughoostos.
settembre.	septembreos.
ottobre.	oktobreos.
novembre.	noembreos.
dicembre.	dekembreos.
I GIORNI DELLA SETTIMANA.	**EEMERE TIS EBDOMADAS.**
domenica.	kiriaki.
lunedi.	devtera.
martedi.	triti.
mercoledi.	tetarti.
giovedi.	pempti.
venerdi.	paraskevi.
sabato.	sabbaton.
LE FESTE.	**EORTI.**
il capo d'anno.	neon etos.
l'epifania.	theofania.

ENGLISH.	TURKISH.
The Carnival.	kàrnavaldir.
Ash Wednesday.	kyùl chìhàrshambèh.
Good Friday.	khàyr jùm''à ghyùni.
Easter.	pàsskàlya.
Whitsuntide.	rùh nùzuli ghyuni.
Christmas.	kùchuk-pàsskàlya.
A month.	bìr àу.
A fortnight.	iki-hàfta.
A week.	bìr hàfta.
To-day.	bìr ghyùn.
Yesterday.	dùn.
The day before yesterday.	dùnki ghyùn.
To-morrow.	yàrin.
The day after to-morrow.	o bìrssi ghyùn.

CHAPTER V.

ASKING AND AFFIRMING.	SORMAK VE TASSDIK ETMEK.
By your leave.	ìzninila, rùkhsàtinizila.
Do me the favour to . . .	bàna kèrem èdiniz.
Might I trouble you to . . .	sìzi zàhmet idèhim . . .
You can render me a great service.	sìz béni bùyuk''ınāyet èdabìlur-siniz.
I am much obliged to you.	sizé chòk màmmūnim.
I thank you most kindly.	tèshèkkyur èderim.
It is not worth noticing.	zìkr òlunmaz.
I am sorry to trouble you so much.	mùté'essifim sìzi chòk zàhmet vèrdim.
I beg you will not mention it.	zàrar yòk.
You are very kind.	pèk mùru'ètlusiniz.
I assure you that . . .	sìze tè'mīn èderim . . .
I say it is not.	sùwèyléimki dèildir.
I suppose so.	sàniderim.
I believe not.	ìnanmam.
Do you think so?	sànidermisiniz.
I think so too.	bèn dàkhi sàniderim.
I must tell you.	sìzè sùwèylèrim.
What do you mean?	né dèmek ìsstérsiniz.

ITALIAN.	GREEK.
il carnavale.	apokreo.
il mercoledì delle ceneri.	kathara tetarti.
il venerdi santo.	meghali paraskevi.
la pasqua.	paskha.
la pentecoste.	pentikosti.
il natale.	khristooghenna.
un mese.	enas minas.
quindici giorni.	dekapente imere.
una settimana.	mia ebdomas.
oggi.	symeron.
jeri.	khthes.
avanti jeri.	prokhthes.
domani.	avrion.
dopo domani.	methavrion.

DOMANDARE ED AFFERMARE.

ETISIS KE BEBIOSIS.

col suo permesso.	me tin adian sas?
mi faccia il piacere di . . .	kamete mi tin kharin . . .
ardirei pregarla . . . ?	mi epitrepete na sas parakaleso.
Potete rendermi un gran servizio.	dinasthe na mi kamite mian ipoorghian.
vi sono molto obligato.	sas ime iperballontos ipokhrios.
vi ringrazio infinitamente.	sas evkharisto kata polla.
non è cosa da parlarne.	ti loghos, ti teriasi.
mi dispiace d'incommodarvi.	me libi to na sas proxesso tosin enokhlisin.
non parlatene vi pregho.	mi anaferete parakalo.
voi siete di gran bontá.	isthe polla kalos.
vi assicuro che . . .	sas bebeo oti . . .
dico di no.	legho legho okhi.
suppongho di si.	to apotheto.
non lo credo.	nomiso okhi.
credete?	nomisete?
credo anch' io.	ki egho to nomiso.
e bene di dirvi.	eene kalon na sas ipo.
che volete dire?	ti thelete na ipite.

ENGLISH.	TURKISH.
It is a fact.	vàk"àdir.
Are you quite sure of it?	ìyi bìlèrminiz.
I am certain of it.	shùbhèssizim.

SURPRISE.	A"JĀY'IB, TA"AJJUB.
What!	nè.
Indeed!	hàkīkàt, ghìrshek.
Is it so?	bùylemi.
Is it possible?	mùmkinmi.
That is impossible.	mùhāl, ghàyri mùmkin.
You surprise me.	béni tà"ajjub ìdiyursiniz.
That is very strange.	a"jà'ibdir.
It was to be expected.	mè'mūl òlajakimish.
I do not wonder at it.	shàshàmeyurum.

SORROW, BLAME.	KEDER VE KABÂHAT.
I am sorry for it.	tè'essuf iderim.
I am quite vexed about it.	chòk ghyùjènirim.
What a pity!	nè yàzik.
It is a great pity.	pèk yàzikdir.
It is a sad thing.	pèk kèderlidir.
That is very disagreeable.	pèk tàtsizdir.
It is very provoking.	kìzdirajakdir.
It is most hard.	pèk àghirdir, mùshkil.
It is a cruel case.	ìnsāniyyètsiz.
It is a great misfortune.	pèk bùyuk bèlādir.
It is terrible.	màkhūfdir.
It is dreadful.	kòrkuludir.
For shame!	"àyb.
Are you not ashamed?	ùtānmazmisin.
You ought to be ashamed?	ùtānmalisin.
It is very bad.	pèk fàna.
How naughty it is!	èdebsizlik.
How can you be so naughty?	nàssl tèrbiyyèsizsin.
How could you do so?	nèya bùylé yàptin.
How came you to do so?	nìchun bùylé yàptin.
You are very much to blame.	kàbāhatlisin.
You are quite wrong.	yānishdasin.
I have no patience with you.	sàna tàhàmmul ètmam.
I am not pleased with you.	sàninila ghòsh dèyilim.

ITALIAN.	GREEK.
è un fatto.	eene gheghonospraghmatikon.
vi siete sicuro?	eesthe peri tootoo bebeos.
sono certo.	eeme pepismenos.

ESPRESSIONI DI SORPRESA.	THAVMASMON APORIAS.
che?	ti?
veramente!	alithia!
davvero?	ne, ne!
è possibile?	eene dinaton!
questo è impossibile.	tou adinaton!
mi maravigliate.	me feris is aporian.
è maravigliosa.	eene poli paradoxon.
d' aspettarsene.	eprepre na to perimeni.
non mi maraviglio.	den thavmaso posos.

AFFLIZIONE E RIMPRO-VERO.	AVSARESTISIS KE APODO-KIMASIA.
mi dispiace.	eeme katapiraghmenos dia tooto.
che peccato!	krima!
è veramenti peccato.	krima toonti.
è gran peccato!	ti kakon!
è cosa dispiacevole.	eene poli disareston.
è cosa disagriabile.	eene poli aneston.
è cosa provocante.	eene lian piraktikon.
è cosa molto dura a sopportare.	eene lian skliron.
è cosa veramente crudele.	eene poli apanthropon.
che schiagura.	eene megha distikhima.
è cosa terribile.	eene tromeron.
è cosa che fa spaventare.	eene tromaktikon toonti.
vergogna!	entropi!
non avete vergogna?	den entrepese?
devete vergognarvi.	eprepe na entrapète.
è veramente male.	eene poli kakon.
che bruta cosa!	ti askhimon!
come potete essere tanto cativo?	pos na isthe toson kakos.
come potete fare ciò?	pos idinithite na kamite tooto?
perche l'avete fatto?	pos to ekamete tooto?
siete molto colpevole.	eesthe poli axiokakritos.
avete gran torto.	ekhete poli adikou.
non ho pazienza con voi.	exantleete tin ipomonin moo.
non mi son contento di voi.	den mevkharistee to fersimon sas.

ENGLISH.	TURKISH.
I shall be very angry.	chòk dàrilirim.
Be quiet.	sùss òl.
Cannot you be still?	ràhāt ùturmazmisin.
I tell you that . . .	sàna sùwèyleyurum.
I will have it.	òf àrtik.
Mind for another time.	"àklda tut bàshka dàfa" íchun.
I am in earnest.	hàkīkat sùwèyliyurum.
Do not do so again.	bàshka dàfa" yàpma.

Chapter VI.

Good morning, Sir.	sabaheniz khair olsun effendim.
How are you to-day?	nasulsiniz bù ghyùn?
I hepe you are well.	inshállah ayusiniz.
I am very well, thank you.	ayuim, tashakkurum.
How is your father?	bederiniz nasel?
How are all at home?	bitun familianiz nasel?
My mother is better to-day.	anam bir-āz ayudir bū ghyun.
She is pretty well.	ayumidir.
She is not very well.	ayudeildir.
My son is ill.	òghlum keȳfsisdir.
My brother is very ill.	karndashim pèk khāssta.
He is dangerously ill.	pèk chok khāsstadir.
My sister is dying.	kiz karindāshim ùlumā yakùndir.
What is the matter with her?	nē-var?
She has a violent cold and fever.	saghuk almish vè setimalider.
I am very sorry to hear it.	té'èssif ederim.
How long has she been ill?	nè-zāmāndan keyfsizdir.
I did not know that she was ill.	belmazidim keyfsizidi.
Does any one attend her?	tabibā ghusterdinizmi?
The doctor comes every day.	hèykim her ghun ghiliur.
He says it is nothing of conse-quence.	zārārsiz demish.
I am very glad.	pèk mèssrūrim.
I must go.	ghèdègagim.
We must part.	ayrilāgiāgiz.
I must take leave of you.	sizden izin alajiagim.

ITALIAN.	GREEK.
sarò rabbiato.	tha disarestitho poli.
statevi quieto.	menete isikhos.
non potete stare quieto?	den isikhasete?
vi dico che . . .	sas simboolevo.
lo voglio.	to thelo.
badate per un altra volta.	prosexate allin feran.
parto davvero.	omilo spoodeos.
non lo fate più.	mi to kamite pleon allote.

buon giorno, signore.	kali imera, kirie.
come sta oggi.	pos evriskesthe simeron?
spero che ella è in buona salute.	elpizo, oti isthe en kali igīa.
sto molto lene, grazie.	evriskome poli kalá.
come sta il signore suo padre?	pos ekhi o kiries patir sas?
come stanno tutti in casa?	pos ekhoosin e eu ti ikia sas?
mia madre è meglio oggi.	i mitir moo iné simerou eligen kalitera.
sta abbastanza bene?	evriskité arketa kalá.
non sta bene.	dén iné toson kalá.
il mio figlio è malato.	pediamoo iné adiathetos.
il mio fratello è malato.	adélfémoo iné asthenis.
è in gran pericolo.	iné epikindinos asthenis.
la mia sorella è moribonda.	adelfamoo telioni.
che ha?	ti ékhi?
ha un gran raffreddore e febre.	ekhi sfodro katarroon ké thermè.
molto mi dispiace.	mi kakofénété poli.
da quando è ammalata.	apo poté asthéni?
non sapeva che fesse ammalata.	den egnorisa oti ito arrestes.
è visitata da qualcuno?	tin pléti kanis.
il dottore viene a vederla ogni giorno.	o iatros erkhété kathiméran is episkepsin tis.
il medico assicura che sarà nulla.	o iatros bébéoni, oti den tha iné tipoté.
mi sono molto contento.	khero dia testo poli.
bisogna che vado.	prépi na ipago.
bisogna seperarci.	prépi na anakhorisomén.
sono obligato di prendere congedo da voi.	prépi na sas apokhérétiso.

ENGLISH.	TURKISH.
Till I have the pleasure of seeing you again.	sizè sèlāmètlān ghùrùngia ākādèr.
Good-bye. Farewell.	āllāh ismārlèdik.
Good-evening. Good-night.	akhshāminiz khāir òlssun.
I wish you good-evening.	ghègjaniz khāir òla.
My compliments to your brother.	pederinizè selām sùileniz.
My kind regards to your sister, your wife.	vālidènizē vè kiz-kharindashinizè selām sùileniz.
Thank you, I will do so.	bāsh ùstunè, tishekkyurim.
Are you hungry? .	àjmisin?
I begin to feel hungry.	kārnim àj.
I have a good appetite.	ishtihām vàr.
What will you take?	nē istermisiniz.
What would you like?	nè bùyùrùrsiniz.
What do you wish to eat?	nè istersiniz yìméyé.
I will take any thing.	nè varisa yerim.
Take some more.	bir-āz dāhā bùyùrùnūz.
Not any more, thank you.	khair tèshekkurum.
Are you thirsty?	sùssùzmisiniz.
What will you drink?	nè itchèrsiniz.
Take a glass of wine.	bir kadeh shārāb buyrunuz.
Give me a glass of water.	bir kadeh sù vèr.
Is there any news to-day?	yèni hāwādiss varmi bù ghyùn?
Is there anything fresh?	tazè hāwādiss varmi.
What is the best news?	nè vàr nè yok.
What news can you tell us?	nè khàber vàr.
Have you anything to tell us?	bir khàberiniz varmi.
What is the talk about town?	charshidé nè lakirdi vàr.
I know nothing new.	bilmam bir sheȳ.
I have not heard of anything.	hitch bir shey ishshitmadim.
The news is good.	khaher ayudir.
There is bad news.	hawadiss fènèdir.
The news is very bad.	hawadis pèk fenedir.
What good news!	nè ghùzel khaber!
I have heard that . . .	ben bùni ishshitim.
I have not heard it spoken of.	ishitmadim.
Did you read the papers?	ghàzèta ùkùdunuzmi.
What do the papers say?	jaridèlerdè ne vàr.
I have not read a paper to-day?	bù ghyùn ghàzèta ùkùmadim.
Did you see that in any paper?	jeridèdèmi ghyurdunuz.

ITALIAN.	GREEK.
finchè abbia il piacere di rivederla.	eos ou bolin labo tin timin na sas idéo.
a rivedervi. addie.	ekhété igian. zas afino igian.
buona sera. buona notte.	kali éspéra. kali nikta.
vi anguro la buona sera.	zas évkhomé kalin éspéran.
i miei complimenti al vostro fratello.	khérétismata is ton kirion adélfon sas.
faccia i miei complimenti alla sua sorella, alla sua madre.	tas prosrisis mon is tin adélfin ké matir sas.
non mancherò di farlo, grazie.	orisnios sas, evkharistó.
avete fame ?	pinatè ?
comincio a sentire fame.	merkhété orèxis.
ho buon appetito.	ekho kalin orèxin.
che cosa mangerete ?	ti tha fagété ?
che cosa volete mangiare ?	ti thélété na fagité ?
che cosa desiderate a mangiare ?	ti epithimété na fagité ?
mangeró qualunque cosa.	trogo o ti tikhi.
piglio di più.	fogété akemi.
nulla più, grazie.	dén thélo plèon tipoté, evkharistó.
avete sete ?	dipsaté ?
cosa volete bevere ?	ti thélété na piité ?
prendete un bicchiere di vine.	parété potirion inen.
datemi un bicchiere d'acqua.	dete mi potirion neró.
vi è novita oggi ?	iné néa siméron ?
vi è qualche cosa di nuove ?	iné ti néon ?
che dicesi di bello ?	ti kalon légété ?
che novità ci dite ?	ti néa tha mas ipètè.
avétè qualche cosa a dirci ?	èkhété ti na mas ipétè ?
che si dice nella cità ?	ti légoon is tin polin ?
non so nulla di nuovo.	dén ixévro eedèn néon.
non ho inteso parlar di nulla.	dén ikoosa na lègoon tipoté.
le novelle son buone.	ta néa iné kalá.
ci son cattivi nuove.	iné kaká ta néa.
le nuove son cattivissime.	ta néa iné poli, kaka.
che buona nuova.	idoo kalon néon.
ho inteso dire che . . .	ikoosa legomènon oti . .
non ne ho inteso parlare.	dén ikoosa na omiloon péri tooto.
avete letto i giornali ?	anégnosaté tis éfiméridas ?
che dicono i giornali ?	ti legoon i éfimerides ?
non ho letto nessun giornale oggi ?	den anégnosa simeron éfimérida ?
lo avete veduto in qualche giornale ?	iddété tooto is kamian éfimérida ?

3

ENGLISH.	TURKISH.
It is only mentioned in a private letter.	yaleniz mektupdè zikr olùnmūsh.
Do they say who received that letter?	bù mèktub kim àlmish sùweyléyurlermi.
Yes, they name the person; it is Mr. S . . .	èvvet, àdamin àdini vèrmishler, filan effendidir.
They greatly doubt the news.	hàwādissa chòk shùbhè ederler.
This news wants confirmation.	bù hàwādiss tàssdík isster.
How do you know that?	bùni nassl bìlirsin.
I give you my authority.	bùrhānimi vèririm.
That report has proved false.	bù tèwātur yalandir.
Do they still talk of war?	kàwgha ùzerinè daha làkirdi idiyurlarmi.
Do they think we shall have peace?	bàrishik òlajakmi zàn íderler.
It is not likely.	mè'mūl déyildir.
Have you heard from your brother?	kàrndàshnizdan khàber varmi.
Have you heard lately from your friend?	dòsstunizdan hàwādissiniz vàrmi.
How long is it since he wrote to you?	chòkdan pèrumi sizè yàzdi.
I have not heard from him these two months.	iki àydan pèru àndan khàbar àlmadim.
He has not written for three weeks.	ùch hàftadan pèru yàzmamish.
I expect a letter from him every day.	àndan bìr mèktub bèkliyurum hèr ghyùn.

GOING AND COMING.

GHETMEK VE GHELMEK.

Where are you going?	nèreya ghìdiyursin.
I am going home.	èvva ghìdiyurum.
I was going to your house.	sìza ghèliyurdim.
Where do you come from?	nèradan ghèliyursin.
I come from my brother's.	kàrendàshimdan ghèliyurim.
I come from church.	kìlīssédan ghèliyurim.
I have just left school.	shìmdi mèktèbi bràktim.
Will you come with me?	bènimila ghelirmisin.
Where do you wish to go?	nèréya istersin ghìtmaga.

ITALIAN.	GREEK.
non se ne parla che in una lettera privata.	monon is idiotikon gramma ginètè mnia tootó.
si dice chi ha ricevuto questa lettera?	ke leghoon píes elabe to ghramma tooto.
si, nominano la persona; è il Signore S . . .	né, onomasoon to prosopoo eene ò Kirie . . .
dubitano questa novità.	amfiballoon poli peri tis alithias tavtis.
questa novità deve essere confirmata.	i idisis tavti khrisis epibebeoseos.
come lo sapete?	pothen to ixevrete?
vi do la mia autorità.	sas leghe pies mi tin eepe.
questo rumore s'é trovato falso.	i fimi avti evrethi oosa psevdis.
si parla ancora di guerra?	omiloon akomi peri polemon?
si crede che avremmo pace?	pistevete oti tha ekhomen irinin?
non è probabile.	den eene pithanon.
avete ricevuto qualche novità dal vostro fratello.	elabete idisis para ton adelfon sas?
avete ricevuto novita ultimamente dal vostro amico?	ine polis keros afoton den elabete idisis para too filoo sas.
quanto tempo fà che vi ha scritto?	posos kiros ine afeton den sas eghrapsen?
sono due mesi che non ho ricevuto novità da lui.	ine dio mines afoton den elaba par' avton kammian idisin.
sono tre settimane che non ha scritto.	pro trien ebdomadon den eghrapse.
aspetto una lettera da lui ogni giorno.	perimeno ghramma ton apo imeras is imeran.

ANDARE E VENIRE.	EPAGHIN KE ERKHESTHE.
dove va? andate?	poo ipaghete?
vado a casa.	ypago is tin ikian.
venivo da voi.	ypighena is esas.
da deve venite?	pothen erkhesthe?
vengo dal mio fratello.	erkhome apo ton adelfon moo.
vengo dalla chiesa.	erkhome apo tin enklisian.
ora ho lasciato la scuola.	exerkhome apo to skolion.
volete venire con me?	thelete na elthite mazimoo?
dove volete andare?	poo thelete na eepaghite?

ENGLISH.	TURKISH.
We will go for a walk.	ghèzmeya ghìderiz.
Willingly.	pèki.
Which way shall we go?	bàngbi yòla ghìderiz.
We will go where you like.	isstadin yèra ghìderiz.
Let us go to the park.	òrmànlik-bàghchaya ghìdelim.
Let us call for your brother on our way.	yòlumisda karndashiniza ghèchelim.
As you like.	nassl istèrsiniz.
Is Mr. B. at home?	felan effendi èvdami.
Can you tell us where he is gone?	bìlirmisiniz nèréya ghìtmish.
He is just gone out.	tàshra chìkmish.
He is not at home.	evda dèyildir.
I think he is gone to see his sister.	sàniderim kiz kàrndashina ghyùrmeya ghìtmish.
Do you knew when he will return?	bìlirmisiniz nàzaman "àvdet èdejak.
No, he did not say anything about it when he went out.	yòk, chìkàrikan bir shei sùwèylamamish.
In that case we must go without him.	pèki, ansiz ghìdelim.

CHAPTER VII.

AGE.	YASH.
What is your age?	nè yàshdassiniz, yàshiniz kàchdir.
How old is your brother?	kàrndashiniz, yàshi kàchdir.
I am twelve years old.	òn ìki yàshliim.
I shall be sixteen next month.	ghèlejak àyda òn àlti yàshinda òlurum.
You do not look so old.	bù kàder yàshlu ghyùrunmazsiniz.
I thought you were older.	sàn ittim zìadè yàshlisiniz.

THE WATCH.	SA"AT.
Do you know what o'clock it is?	sà"at kàchdir bilirmisiniz.
I cannot tell you exactly.	tamàm wàkti siza diyamam sàhìhan bìlmiyurim.
Look at your watch.	sà"atiniza bàkiniz.
It is not wound up.	kùrulmamishdir.
I forgot to wind it up.	kùrmaghi ùnùttim.
It does not go.	ishlàmeyur.

ITALIAN.	GREEK.
anderemmo a passegiare.	tha eepaghomen (is) peripaton.
volentieri.	evkharistos.
da qual parte anderemo?	pothen tha eepaghomen?
anderemmo dove volete.	eepaghomen opoo thelete.
andiamo al parco.	as eepaghomen ees ton kipon.
prendiamo il vostro fratello con noi.	as simbasalabomen ton adelfonsas.
come volete.	opos thelete.
il Signor B. è in casa?	o Kirie eene is tin eekian?
potete dirci dove è andate?	eexevrete na me eepite poo eepighe?
è uscito peco fà.	pro olighoo exilthen.
lui non è in casa.	den eene is tin eekian.
credo che sia andato a vedere la sua sorella.	nomiso oti eepighen is episkefin tis adelfis too.
sapete quando ritornerà?	eexevrete pote tha epistrepse.
no, non ha detto niente quando sorti.	okhi, den eepe tipota anakhoron.
va bene, anderemo senza lui.	leepon, tha eepaghomen khoris avton.

Chapter VII.

ETA.	EELIKIA.
che età avete?	ti eelikian ekhete?
che età ha il vostro fratello?	ti eelikias eene adelfos sas?
ho dedici anni.	ceme dedeka eten.
avrò sedici anni nel mese prossime.	ton prosekhi mina ghinome dekaex eten.
non apparite tanto vecchio.	den fenesthe ekhon tosin eelikian.
vi credeva più vecchie.	sas enomisa pleon eelikiomenon.

L'OROLOGIO.	TO OROLOGION.
sapete che ora é?	ixevrete ti ora eene.
non posso dirvelo esatamente.	den eemboro na sas to eepo kat' akribeean.
guardate al vostro orologio.	idate to orologion sas.
non è carice.	den eene koordismenon.
ho dimenticato di caricarla.	elismonisa na to koordiso.
non va.	den pighenee.

ENGLISH.	TURKISH.
It has stopped.	dùrmishdir.
What o'clock is it by yours?	sìzinsā"atinizkàcha ghyùstariyur.
Does yours go well?	sizinki dòghru ghìdiyurmi.
Mine does not go well.	bènimki dòghru ghìtmiyur.
It is not right.	dòghru dìghildir.
It is too fast.	ìléridir.
It is too slow.	ghéri.
It is out of order.	bùzulmishdir.
It stops now and then.	bà"zi kèrrè dùriyur.
It loses a quarter of an hour every day.	hèr ghyùn bìr chèyrek ghèri kaléyur.
It gains half an hour every day.	hèr ghyùn yārim sā"àt ìlèri ghìdiyur.
Something in it is out of order.	ìchinda bìr shèy bòzmishdir.
Something is broken.	ìchinda bir shèy kìrilmishdir.
The mainspring is broken.	zèmberèk kírilmishdir.
I think the chain is broken.	zān ìderim zìnjiri kìrilmishdir.
You must get it mended.	tā"mīr ìdiniz.
I am going to send it to the watch-maker.	sā"atjiya ghyùnderejaghim.
It is mid-day, twelve o'clock.	ghyùnduzòrtassi sū"àt on ìki.
It is not yet two o'clock.	sā"àt iki dàha òlmadi.
It is twenty minutes past four.	dùrta yìghirmi ghèchdi.
It is not late.	ghèj dèghildir.
The clock strikes.	mèydan-sā"àti chàliyur.

CHAPTER VIII.

VISIT.	ZIYARET.
There is a knock.	kàpi chàlinyur.
Some one rings.	bìrissi chìngharàghi chàliyur.
Go and see who it is.	ghìdub ghyùriniz kimdir.
Go and open the door.	ghìdiniz kàpiyi àchiniz.
Good morning, Mr. S.	sàbāh shèrìfleriniz khàyr òlsum effendim.
I am very glad to see you.	sisléré ghyùrdighumdan pèk memnùn òldum.
I have not seen you for a long time.	chòk vàkitdirki sisléré ghyùramadim.
You are quite a stranger.	bìtun sìslèr èjnébi òldiniz.

ITALIAN	GREEK.
s'é fermato.	estathi.
che ora è al vostro.	ti eran leghee to idikon sas.
il vostro è va bene.	pighenee kala to idikon sas.
il mio non va bene.	to edikon moo den pighanee kala.
non idica bene il tempo.	den pighenee ertha.
avanza.	pighenee embros.
ritarda.	pighenee opiso.
è guasto.	eene khalasmenon.
si ferma alcuni volte.	stekee ek dialeemmaton.
perdi un quarto d'ora ogni giorno.	kath'ekastin imeran menee opiso en tetarton tis oras.
avanza mezza ora ogni giorno.	kath'ekastin imeran pighenee embros imiseean oran.
vi è qualche cosa guastate.	kati ekhalase.
forse qualche cosa è rotto.	kati etsakisthi.
la molla è rotta.	to elatirion ethravsthi.
credo che la catena è rotta.	nomiso oti i alisos ekoti.
fatelo aggiustare.	prepee na diorthothè.
va mandarlo al orologiaio.	tora tha tin seelo ees ton orologhan.
è mezzogiorno.	eene dedeka, mesimeri.
non son ancora le due ore.	den eene akemi dio.
sono lequatro e venti.	eene tessares ke eekosi lipta.
non è tardi.	den eene argha.
ecce l'orologio suona.	idoo ktita to orologion.

Chapter VIII.

LA VISITA.	EE EPISKEPSIS.
si picchia.	ktipa tis.
qualcheduno suona.	koodoonisee tis.
andate a vedere chi é.	idite piós eene.
andate aprire la porta.	anixate tin thiran.
buon giorno, Signore S.	sas evkhome kalin imeran.
ho molto piacere di vederla.	kalos orisate.
non vi ho veduto da molto tempo.	af' otoo den sas eeda.
voi siete divenuto stragnero.	eesthe toson spanios os e kale imere.

ENGLISH.	TURKISH.

Pray sit down.
Give a chair to Mr. S.
I cannot stay.
I only called to inquire after you.

I must go.
You are in a great hurry.
I have much to do.
I will stay longer another time.
I hope I shall soon see you again.

kèrem ìdub òturiniz effendim.
effendiya bir sàndālìyyé vèr.
kàlamam.
fàkat sizléri ziyārèt ètmaya ghél-
dim.
ghétmaluim.
pèk tà"jīl ìdiyursiniz.
chòk ìshim vàrdir.
bàshka dèf"à chòk èylenirim.
mè'mūl yàkinda effendimi tèkrār
ghyùrurim.

BREAKFAST.

Have you breakfasted?
Not yet.
You are just in time.
You will breakfast with us.
Do you drink tea or coffee?

Would you prefer chocolate?
Here are rolls and toast.
I prefer a piece of toast.

You have not enough milk.
Allow me to pour out some more.
Make yourself at home.

KAHWALTI.

kàhwàlti èttinizmi.
khàyr dàka ètmadim.
tàmām wàkitinda ghèldiniz.
bìsimila kàhwàltiya bùyuriniz.
kàhwàmi yòkhsa chàymi icher-
siniz.
chìkolàta tèrjīh èdersiniz.
ìshta fìrànjila vè kìzàrmish ekmek.
bèn kìzàrmish èkmeki tèrjīh
èdermi.
sùdiniz kyāfī dèghildir.
ìhsān ìdub bìr-àz dàha sud àliniz.
kèndi èviniz ghìbi tèklīfsiz òluniz.

DINNER.

At what time do we dine to-day?

We are to dine at four o'clock.

We shall not dine until five.

Shall we have anybody at dinner?

I expect Mr. . . .
Mr. D. has promised to come if
the weather permit.

· AKHSHAM-YEMEGHI.

bù ghyùn sā"àt kachdè tà"ām
edahjaghiz.
sā"àt dùrtteh tà"ām edajaghiz.

bèshdan èvvel tà"ām etmayaja-
ghiz
bù ghyùn tà"āmda mùssāfiriniz
vārmi?
fìlan effendīī ùmīdr (ùmùt)ederim.
ègher hàwanin vwùrss"àti òluzissa
fìlan effendi dàkhi ghèlirim
dèyu vwà"d itti.

ITALIAN.	GREEK.
vi pregho di sedere.	kathisate sas parakalo.
date una sedia al Signore.	dete mian kathiklan ees to Kirien.
non posso restare.	den eemboro na meene.
sono venuto solamente di domandare come stà.	iltha monon die na sas ido pos eesthe.
devo andare.	prepee na ipagho.
siete in grande premura.	eesthe poli biastiki.
ho melte cose da fare.	ekho pola ergha na kame.
resteró piú lungo un altra volta.	allote kathime perissoteron.
spero di rivederla presto.	elpiso na sas xanedo takheos.

LA COLAZIONE.

TO PROGHEVMA.

avete fatto colazione?	eproghevmatisate.
non ancora.	okhi akomi.
siete justamente in tempo.	erkhesthe ees tin oran.
farete colazione con noi.	tha proghevmatisate masi mas.
bevete té ovvero caffè?	pernete té ee kafen.
preferisca la cioccolata?	mi thelete kallitera sokolatan.
ecco panetti e pane arostito.	idoo psomakia ke psomioo kavta.
preferisco un pezzo di pane rostito.	pretino mian frèghanian.
non avete latte abbastanza.	den ekhete arketon ghala.
mi permetta di versarvi ancora.	epitrepsate mi na sas bale akemi.
faccia come se fesse in casa sua.	kamete oran na isthe ees tin ikian sas.

PRANZO.

TON GHEVMATOS.

a che ora pranziamo oggi?	ti oran ghevmatizomen simeron?
dobbiamo pranzare alle quatro?	prepī na ghevmatizomen īs tas tessaras.
non pranzeremmo prima delle cinque.	den tha ghevmatisomen proton pente.
avremo qualche d'uno a pranzo oggi?	tha ekhomen kanena simerou is to ghevma.
aspetto il Signore . . .	perimeno ton Kirie . . .
il Signore D. ha promesso di venire se il tempo lo permette.	ò Kirie D. ipeskethi na elthé an ò keros to sinkhorisi.

ENGLISH.	TURKISH.
What shall we have for dinner?	yèmek itchùn nè ìssmārlayalim?
Shall we have fish?	bàlik issmàrlayalimmi?
I could not get any fish.	bàlik bùlmadim.
There was no fish in the market.	bāzārda bàlik yòkidi.
I fear we shall have a poor dinner.	kòrkarím tà''āmimiz pèk sādé òlajakdir.
We must do as well as we can.	ìmkyāni mèrtébé tàmām òlmassiné sàií ètmaluiz.
Will you take some soup?	chòrbadan bir āz bùyururmisiniz?
Thank you, I prefer beef.	khayr effendim sìghir èti ìnāyet bùyriniz.
It looks very good.	ò pèk ā''là ghyùrinur.
Which cut do you prefer?	kànghi (hànghi) tàrafini sèversiniz?
How shall I cut it?	kànghi (bàngbi) tàrafdan kèséyìm?
Will you have it well or under done?	pìshmìshdan mi yokhsa pìshmamishdan mi bàzz èdàrsiniz.
Well done, if you please.	pìshmish tàrafindan ìhsān bùyurun.
Under done, if you please.	pìshmamishdan kèrem bùyuruniz.
I hope this is as you like.	mè'mūl ìdèrim bù pàrcha effendimin bàzz ettiklari ghibidir.
It is excellent.	à''làdan à''là.
Now I am going to send you a piece of pie.	sizè shimdi (shìndi) bir-āz bùrekindan ghyùnderejaghim.
Do you like fat?	yàgh sèvermisiniz.
I prefer some of the lean?	bir-āz yàghsiz tàrafindan kèrem ìdèniz.
A little of each.	bir āzzejik ìkisindandè ìsstérim.
You have no gravy.	èt sùiniz yokdir.
I have plenty, thank you.	tìshèkkyur ìderim ìsstedighimdan zìyādédir.
How do you like the kibab?	kèbābi nassl bùlyùrsiniz.
Shall I help you to some vegetables?	sìzé bir-āz sèbyéwàt (zèrzéwāt) vèraimmi.
You have not any sauce.	tà''ām tèrbìyyéniz yòkdir.
Here are spinage and broccoli.	ishta ísspànak ìshta làhana.
Will you have peas or cauliflower?	bèzèliami yòkhsa kárnabìtmi isstersiniz.
These French beans are excellent.	bù fāssulia pèk àladir.

ITALIAN.	GREEK.
che cosa avremo per il pranzo?	ti tha ekhomen dia to ghevma mas?
avremo pesce?	tha ekhomen psari?
non ho potuto ottenire pesce.	den īmboresa na evre psari.
non vi era pesce nel mercato.	oode en psari den ito īs tin agoran.
ho paura che avremo un povero pranzo.	foboome tos tha ekhomen distikhimenon ghevma.
faremo come potremo.	as perasomen òpos īmporesomen.
la vuele della suppa?	pernete sooppan?
grazie, preferisco un po' di manzo.	evkharisto, tha sas zitiso eligen bodinon.
mi pare che è molto buona.	fenete toson kalon.
di qual parte vi piacerà piu?	ti meros protinate?
da qual parte lo taglierò?	àpo ti meros na to kopso?
lo vuol ben o meno cotto?	to thelete kalokrasmenon i ologon brasmenon.
mi favorirà del ben cotto.	kalo brasmenon parakalo.
mi favorirà meno cotto.	òkhi parapoli brasmenon, parakalo.
spero che questo pezzo sia del suo gusto.	elpizo to komati tooto na īne tis erekseos sas.
è eccellente.	īne eksèreton.
ora le darò un pezzo di questo pasticcio.	tosa tha sas stīlo en kommati apo tooto to pastitzo (tavtin tin pittan).
vi piace il grasso?	àghapate to pakhi?
preferisco un po' di magro.	dote mi psakhnon, parakalo.
un poco dell' uno e dell' altro.	òlighon ke apo ta dio.
non avete sugo.	den ekhete zomon zoomi.
mille grazie ne ho abbastanza.	evkharistò ekho arketon.
come vi piace il kibab?	pos sas fenete to kibab?
posso offrirla dei legumi?	na sas prosfero laksanika?
non avete salsa.	den ekhete saltsan.
eccoli spinaci e broccoli.	idoo spanakia ke improkola.
volete piselli o cavolifiori.	thelete mpiselia i koonoobidia?
questi faginoli sono eccellenti.	avta ta fasolia eene exereta.

ENGLISH.	TURKISH.
You have not tasted the artichokes.	ìnghinārdan tàtmadiniz.
Do you like salad?	salatadan bùyururmisiniz.
Here are potatoes and cabbage.	ìshta yèr-èlmassi vè làhana.
Will you take white or brown bread?	fìrànjilami yokhsa èssmèr ekmekmi ìsstersiniz.
It is quite the same to me.	bàna hèp bìrdir.
Shall I help you to a little of this?	sizi bùndan bìr-àz vīreimme.
Allow me to give you some.	rùkhsatiniz ila bùndan bìr-àz sizé vīreimme.
Shall I send you a slice of this leg of mutton?	bù kòyun bùdindan siza bìr-àz vīreimme.
It seems excellent.	pèk àla ghyùriniur.
It is very juicy.	pèk sùludir.
You have not eaten any pudding.	bùdinidan tàtmadiniz.
This fricandeau is delicious.	bù frìkandu pèk lèzīz.
Shall I help you to some?	àndan bir-àz siza vèraimme.
I will thank you for a very small piece, just to taste it.	hèmān tàtajak kàdr kèrem ìdin.
Give me very little.	àz bìr shèy "ìnāyet boyùrun.
You eat nothing.	hìeh bìr shèy yèmiyùrsiniz.
I beg your pardon, I have done very well.	"àfv ìdiniz pèk àla yèyurim.
Now, what can I offer you?	shimdi effendim siza ne tàklīf idaim.
I will send you a piece of this fowl.	bù tàwukdan bìr-az siza vèraim.
Not any more, thank you.	àrtik bìr shèy ìsstémem effendim.
A little fowl cannot hurt you.	bìr pàrcha tàwuk sizé iǹjitmaz.
Kindly give me a very small piece.	pék jùz'ī bìr pàrcha ìhsān ìdiniz.
Bring the gentleman a plate.	effendiya bìr tàbak ghètur.
Which do you like, a leg or a wing?	kànadmi yòkhsa bùtmi sèversiniz.
It is all the same to me.	bènja hànghisi òlsa bìr dir.
You give me too much.	pèk chòk vèrdiniz.
Kindly give me half.	ànin yàrisini vèriniz.
Cut that in two.	àni ìkiya bùleniz.
Half of it will be enough.	yàrisi bàna kyāfīdir.

ITALIAN.	GREEK.
non avete gustato i carciofi.	den eghevthite tos anghinaras.
mangiate salata.	troghete salatan ?
eccoli patate e cavoli.	idoo gheomila ke krambolakhana.
prendete pane bianco ovvero bigio?	thelete psomi levkon i apo to devteren.
per me è la stessa cosa.	mi eene odiaforon.
posso offrirla un pezzo di questo?	orisete en komation apo tooto.
permettetemi di darvi un pezzo.	dete mi tin adeean na sas prosfero en temkhion apo tooto.
desidera che vi mando un pezzo della coscia di mottone?	na sas seele en temakhion apo tooto to podori.
pare eccelente.	fenete exereton.
è molto sugoso piene di sugo.	eene evkhimotaton.
non avete mangiate podino.	den efaghete poodingan.
queste bracinole di vitello sono bueni.	tooto to ghiakhni eene nostimotaton.
posso offrirla peco ?	nasas prosfero apo tooto ?
mi favorirà un pezzo per gustarla.	parakalo en mikrotaton temakhion, oson monen na to dokimaso.
datemi un peco solamente.	olighon monen dote mee.
voi non magiate niente.	sees den troghete tipote.
mi perdoni, ho magiato molto bene.	me singkhoreete, trogho poli kala.
ora che posso offrirla.	tora ti ara ghe na sas prosfero.
vi manderò un pezzo di questa gallina.	as sas steelo en kommation apo ta pavlerika avta.
mille grazie, non più.	sas evkharisto den tha fagho pleon allo.
un pezzo di gallina non vi farà del male.	en kommataki poolioo den tha sas plaxee.
digrazia mi manda un piccolo pezzo.	dote mi lipen en polla mikron kommati.
portate un piatto al signore.	fere en pinakion ees ton kiron.
quale vi piace della coscia, ovvero dell'ala?	ti prokrinete, kopanon i fteroogha.
per me è tutto lo stesso.	mi eene to idion.
m'avete dato troppo.	mi didete para poli.
di grazia datemi la metà solamente.	mi dosite para to imisi.
dividete queste in due.	khorisate to ees dio.
la metà mi basterebbe.	to imisi arkee.

ENGLISH.	TURKISH.
So? Will that do?	shùylémi.
Thank you, there is plenty.	èvet effendim bàna yètishir.
You may clear away.	sòfrayi kàldir.
Take away, and bring some wine.	sòfrayi kàldir vè bir-àz shàrab ghètir.

Chapter IX.

TEA.	CHAY.
Have you carried in the tea things?	chày tàkimini ìchèri ghètirdinme.
Everything is on the table.	her bìr shèy sòfra ùzérindadir.
Does the water boil?	sù kàynayurmi.
Tea is quite ready.	chày hāzirdir.
They are waiting for you.	sizé bèkliyurler.
I am coming.	ghèliyurim.
I follow you.	àrkaniz sòngra ghèliyurim.
You have not put a basin on the table.	sòfraya kyāssé kòmamishsin.
We have not cups enough.	fìnjānimiz èkzikdir.
We want two more cups.	iki fìnjān dàha ìsteriz.
Bring another spoon and a saucer.	bìr kàshik dàha vèbirdé bìr finjàn tàbaki ghètir.
You have not brought the sugar-tongs.	shèker màshasini ghètirmamish-sin.
Do you take sugar?	chày shèkerlu ìchermisiniz.
Do you take cream?	kàymaklan ìchermisiniz.
I will thank you for a little more milk.	bìr-àz dàha sùd "ināyet idiniz.
The tea is very strong.	chày pèk kùvvetlidir.
I can give you more.	bìr-àz dàha vèrayim.
We have plenty.	sùdiniz chòkdir.
Do not spare it.	idārélu kùllanmaniz.
Here are cakes and buttered rolls.	ìshté kùrabiyéìshté yàghli fìrànjila.
Do you prefer bread and butter?	tàréyàghila èkmeki tèrjìh ìder-misiniz.
Get more bread and butter.	bìr-àz dàha tèréyàghila ekmek ghètir.
Hand me the plate.	tàbaki bàna vèr.
Permit me to offer you some cake.	rùkhsàtinizla siza kùrabiyé vèreim.

ITALIAN.	GREEK.
come. cosí?	pos?
grazie, abbastanza.	evkharisto idoo toson arkee.
potete portare via.	dinasthe na sikosite ta faghita.
prendete via e portateci il vino.	sikosate ta foghita ke ferete mas krosi.

IL TE.

TO TE.

avete portate tutte le cose per il té?	eferete ola ta khreeodi dia to té?
tutte, signore, è sulla tavela.	ta panta eene epi tis trapesis.
l'acqua bolle?	brasee to neron?
il té è pronto.	to té eene etimon.
vi aspettano.	sas perimenoon.
vengo.	erkhome.
vi seguo.	sas akolootho.
non aveta messo la tazzone sulla tavela.	den ebalete lekanin epi tis trapesis.
non abbiamo tazze abbastanza.	den eene arketis tassis fialia.
vogliamo ancora due chicchere.	khreeasometha akemi dio tassis.
portateci ancora cucchiaio e una sotto tazza.	ferete akemi en khooliarion ke en piatellon.
non avete portato le mollette di zuccharo.	den eferete tin sakharaghran (tsimpida).
prende zuccharo?	thelete sakharin?
prende di crema?	thelete kaimaki?
mi favorisca ancora un poco di latte.	ithela akemi olighon ghala.
il té è molto forte.	to té eene poli dinato.
posso darvi di più.	na sas doso pleeoteron.
abbiamo molto.	ekhomen afthonon.
non lo risparmiate.	mi to lipeeste.
eccolo galletti e focacie.	idoo plakoontia ke pittes.
preferite fette di pane con butirro?	protimate fettes fomioo me bootiron.
portate ancora pane con butirro.	ferete akemi olighon fosnion me bootiron.
passatemi il piatto.	ferete edothen to pinakion.
mi permetta d'offrirvi di galletti?	dote mi tin adian na sas prosfero pittan.

ENGLISH.	TURKISH.
Shall I help you to some cake?	bù kùrabiyadan bìr-àz siza vère-imme.
Give me a small piece, please.	bìr-àz mìkdār "ìnāyet ìdiniz.
Allow me to cut you another piece.	rùkhsát vèrin siza bìr-àz dàha vèreim.
Not any more, thank you.	khàyr effendi àrtik èlverir.
Would you rather not?	sàhīhmi dìyùrsiniz.
Ring the bell, if you please.	kèrem ìdub chìngharaghi chàliniz.
Will you have the goodness to ring the bell?	"ìnāyet ìdub chìngharaghi chà-liniz.
We want more water.	bìza bìr-àz dàha sù làzimdir.
Make more toast.	dàha èkmek kìzàrt.
Bring it in as soon as possible.	ìmkyāni mèrtébé chàbik ghètir.
Make haste.	chàbik òl.
Take the plate with you.	tàbaghi bèrābèr ghyùtur.
Ladies, is the tea as you like?	hànim effendiler chày ìstedughiniz ghibidir.
Is your tea sweet enough?	chàyniz shèkeri kyāfīmidir.
Have I put sugar enough in your tea?	chàyniza mìkdār kìfāye shèker kòymishmi'im.
I do not like it quite so sweet.	òlkader tàtli hàzz ètmam.
Your tea is very good.	pèk àla chàyniz vàr.
Where do you buy it?	bù obàyi kimdan àliyursiniz.
I buy it at . . .	fèlan yèrdan àlirim . . .
It is the best shop for coffee and tea.	kàhwé ve chày ìchin bìrinji dùk-kyāndir.
You have a pretty tea service.	birpék ghyùzèl chày tàkiminiz vardir.
The tea pot is very handsome.	chày ìbrighi pèk làtīfdir.
The sugar basin and milk jug, too, are very pretty.	sùd kàbila shèker kyāsséssila ghāyetla zàrīfdir.
Have you finished already?	hàman bìtirdinizmi.
Do take another cup?	bìr fìnjān dàha bùyuriniz.
Let me give you half a cup?	yàrim fìnjan dàha siza chày vère-jàghim.
You cannot refuse me.	béni dèrīgh ìdamazsiniz.
No, thank you; I would rather not.	zìadehsila tèshèkkyur ìderim àrtik ìchmem.

ITALIAN.	GREEK.
posso offrirvi un pezzo di galletti?	na sas prosfero en temakhion pittas?
vi pregho di favorirmi un poco.	dote mi en kommataki an evarestisthe.
permettetemi di tagliarvi ancora un altro pezzo.	singhkhorisate mi na sas kopso allo en temakhion.
non più, mille grazie.	sas evkharisto kata polla.
senza ceremonia.	mi sistellesthe.
vi pregho di suonare la campana.	ktipisate ton kodona parakalo.
volete aver la bontà di suonare la campana?	labete tin kalosinin na simanete?
vogliamo ancora dell'acqua.	khreeosometha akemi neron.
fate ancora del pane rosto.	tisate akoma merikes fettes fomioo.
portategle il più presto possibile.	ferete tas takhista.
fate presto.	spevsate. oghlighora.
prendete il piatte con voi.	parete masi sas to pinakion.
signore, il té è del loro gusto?	kirie eene to té kata tin orexin sas?
il lore té è dolce?	ekhee to té sas arketin zakharin?
ho messo zuccharo abbastanza nel té.	ebala arketin zakharin ees to té sas.
non mi piace molto dolce.	den to aghapo para poli glikon.
il vostro té è molto bono.	to té sas eene poli kalon.
dove lo comprate?	poo to aghorasete?
lo compro da . . .	to aghorazo ees too . . .
è la migliore botega per cafe e té.	eene to kalliteron erghastirion dia to teeon ke ton kafen.
avete bel servizio di tavela.	ekhete kallisten serbitsion.
il vaso del té è molto belle.	ee tee era eene lian filokalos kateskevasmeni.
anche la zuccheriera e il vase di latte sono molti belli.	ee sakharothiki ke to annghion too ghalaktos eene evmorfotata.
avete finito già?	eleleeofate idi?
prenderete ancora un altra tazza.	tha parete akemi enpotirion.
vi verseró una mezza tazza.	tha sas pale akemi mison tassan.
non mi rifuterà.	den tha mi to apopeethite.
no, mille grazie.	sas evkharisto miriakis (khilia spolati).

ENGLISH.	TURKISH.
### SUPPER.	### GHEYJE-YEMEGHI.

Do stay and sup with us.	bìzimila ghèyjé yèmèghina kàlir-misiniz.
Thank you much, but I fear it will be too late.	effendima tèshèkkyur ìderim làkin ghèch kalirim kòrkarim.
We shall have supper directly.	haman shìmdi ghèyjé tà‘‘āmi ìdajàghiz.
A little bread and cheese will do well.	bàna èkmek pènir kyāfīdir.
We shall have some cold meat and a few oysters.	bìr-àz sòghuk èt ve bir kàch ìsstridiyadan ‘‘ìbāretdir.
Do you like oysters?	ìsstridiya sèvermisiniz.
I like them very much.	ziadehsila sèverim.
I will send for some, and we will sup immediately.	bìr-àz ghètirsinler dé dir ‘‘àkab tà‘‘ām ìderiz.
Here are ham and cold beef, which may I offer you first?	èvvélā siza né‘‘àrz ìduim, ìshtè sòghuk sìghir èti ishté dònguz bùdi bàssdirmasi.
I will take some oysters.	bìr kàch tāné ìsstridiya yèrim.
How do you like them?	ànnlari nàssl bèghendiniz.
They are quite fresh.	tāzémidir.
They are very good.	pèk àyidir.
Will you take a few more?	bìr kàch tāné dàha àlmazmisiniz.
No, thank you, I will take a little ham.	khàyr effendim bèndéniza bìr-àz dòrnūz èti kèrem ìdiniz.
Give me very little.	jùz‘i bìr pàrsha ìhsān ìdiniz.
Will you have a piece of this apple tart?	bù èlma bùrekindan ìstermisiniz.
It looks good.	Ayija ghyùrinyur.
I cannot take anything more.	àrtik bìr shèy yèyèmam.
Will you take a glass of wine with me?	bènimila bìr kàdeh shàrab bùyu-rurmisiniz.
Willingly, thank you.	mèmnūn òlurim effendim.
Which do you prefer, red or white?	kìrmizi shàrabini yòkhsa bèyāzin-mi tèrjīh ìdersiniz.
I prefer white.	bèyāz tèrjīh ìderim.
Bring two glasses of wine.	ìki kàdeh shàrab ghètir.
Your health, Sir!	sìhhàtiniza effendim
Give me a glass of water, if you please?	bìr kàdeh sù kèrem ìdiniz.

ITALIAN.	GREEK.
## LA CENA.	## TO DEEPNON.

ITALIAN.	GREEK.
volete cenare con noi?	menete na deepnisomen omoo?
vi ringrazoi, ma temo che sarà tardi.	sas eeme apokhreos, alla foboome mi eene parapoli argha.
ceneremmo subito.	tha deepnisomen ameses.
pane e formaggio basterà.	psomi ke tiri arkee.
avremo solamente un po' di carne fredo con estriche.	tha ekhomen monon olighon krion kreas ke merika ostreedia.
vi piacce l'ostriche.	aghapate ta ostreedia?
mi piacciono molto.	poli ta aghapo.
manderò a pigliar subito e ceneremo.	tha steele lipon na sitisoon ke tha deepnisomen amesos.
ecco prosciutto e manzzo freddo, che vi darò prima?	idoo khiromeri ke bodinon krien, ti proton na sas prosfero.
mangierò alcuni estriche.	tha fagho oligha ostreedia.
come vi piaceno?	pos sas fenonte?
sono fresche?	eene prosfata?
sono buonissime.	eene poli kala.
non prendete ancora due o tre?	den pernete akomi dio tria?
no grazie, prenderó un peco di prosciutto.	okhi sas evkharistó, tha paro de me tin adeean sas oligho khiromeri.
datemi un poco.	dotemi alla polla olighon.
volete un pezzo di questa torta di pomo.	thelete en kommati apo tavtin tin milopittan.
pare molto buona.	fenete kamposon kali.
non prende più nulla.	den tha paro pleon tipote.
volete prendere un bicchiere di vino con me?	thelete na piomen omoo en potirion inoo.
grazie, volentieri.	meta kharas, asmenos.
quale desiderate del nero o del bianco.	thelete kokkinon ee aspron.
favoritemi del bianco.	perno aspron, an aghapate.
portate due bicchieri di vino.	ferete dio potiria inoo.
alla vestra salute, Signore.	ees eeghian sas, Kirie.
datemi un bicchiere di acqua, se vi piace.	dotemi en potirion neró para kalo.

CHAPTER X.

MARKETING.	PAZAR HAKINDADIR.
We must go to the market.	pàzàra ghètmaluiz.
Will you inquire the price of ducks and fowls to-day?	bàk ùrdek ve tàwuk bù ghyùn kàcha sàtilir.
Try to get a couple of fine fowls.	ìki tàné tàwuk àlmagha bàk.
Do you want any eggs?	yìmurta ìsstérmisiniz.
Yes, buy some eggs and some butter.	èvvet bìr kàeh yìmurtaila bìr-àz tère yàghi àl.
Take three pounds, if it be good.	ègher àla issa ùch kìyyè àl.
As you go to market, call at the butcher's.	pàzàra ghìderikan kàssabada òghra.
What meat shall I order to-day?	bù ghyùn né èt ìssmarlayim.
A neck of mutton and a leg of lamb.	bìr kòyun bòyunila bìr kùzu bùt.
Ask him if he has a good sweet-bread.	àna sù'àl èt ki bìr àyi bùzaghi bèyzi vàrmi.
If he has not, get it elsewhere.	ègher àuda yòkissa sā'ir yèrdan àl.
See if he has an ox tongue.	bàk ànda bìr ghyùzèl sìghir dìl vàrmi.
Let him send it directly.	àni der "àkab ghyùndersin.
Tell him to send the bill with it.	àna sùwèyla hìssābinida àninila bèrābèr ghyundersin.
Have you been to the fish market?	bàlik pàzàrina ghìttinmi.
I have just come from it.	shùndi òradan ghèliyùrim.
Is there much fish?	bàlik vàrmi.
There is very little fish to-day.	bù ghyùn pèk àz bàlik vàr.
There is plenty of fish to-day.	bù ghyùn pèk chòk bàlik vàr.
There is a full market.	pàzàr dòludir.
What kind of fish is there?	né júnss bàlik vàr.
There are herrings and whiting.	lòfār vàr kèfal vàr.
There are soles, turbot, and plenty of mackerel.	dìl bàlighi kàlkan bàlighi vè bìr chòk ùsskùmru vàr.
Did you ask the price of the mackerel?	ùsskùmrunin bàhāssi sòrdinizmi.
The price varies with the size.	jèssāmètina ghyùré sàtilir.
Is there any shell-fish?	bùjek bàlik vàrmi.

COMPRARE.	PERI AGHORAS.
dobiamo andore al mercato.	prepee na ipaghomen ees tin aghoran.
domandate quante costano le anetre e galline.	idete ti timin ekhoon e nisse ke ta poolia.
circate di portare due buoni galline.	prospathisete na evrite dio kalas poelias.
volete uove?	thelete avgha.
si comprate uove e butirro.	malista aghorasete avgha ke bootiron.
prendete tre libbre s'é buone.	parete trees lipras, an ine kalon.
andando al mercato passate dal beccaio.	pighenontes ees tin aghoran perasete apo ton kreopolin.
qual carne ordinerò oggi?	ti kreas na parangheelo simeron.
un collo di mottone ed una coscia d'agnello.	en kommati lemoo kriarioo ke en mirion arnioo.
domandategli se ha buone animelle di vitello.	erotisate ton an ekhi kalas gharghalithras moskharioo.
se non le ha prendeteli altrove.	an den ekhi parete ap' alloo.
vedete se ha una buona lingua di bove.	kittoxata, an ekhi mian kalin bodinin ghlossan.
che la mandi subito.	as ta steeli parevthis.
ditegli che mandi la lista conto, anche.	eepete too na steeli ke ton loghariasmon.
siete andato al mercato di pesce?	ipighete ees ta psaradika.
adesso vengo di lá.	ap' ekec erkhome.
ce ne pesce?	eene psaria.
ce ne peco di pesce oggi.	oligha psaria eene simeron.
ce ne molto pesce oggi.	eene poli psari simerou.
il mercato è pieno.	eene pola kali psariki.
che specie di pesce ce ne?	ti eedos opsaria eene.
ci sono aringhe ed aselli.	eene renghes ke ghadi.
ci sono sogliole, rombi, e grande quantità di sgombri.	eene ghlosse, rombi ke megha posen skombrion.
avete domandato il prezo dei sgombri?	erotisate tin timin ton skombrion?
si vendono secondo la grossezza.	poloonte kata to meghethos.
vi sono conchiglie?	eene konkhilia?

ENGLISH.	TURKISH.
There are shrimps, crabs, and a few lobsters.	tèké vàr yènghèchila isstàkoz vàr.
What time would you like dinner?	tà"āmi né vàkit ìsstersiniz.
Let us have it at six.	sà"āt àltida vèriniz.
Let dinner be ready by six o'clock.	sà"āt àltida tà"ām hàzir òlsun.
Let us have macaroni and pilaf.	màkàrna vè pèlāf vèrèniz.
We will have some tomatoes.	bìr-àz tomatos bìza bèr.

WALKING.   GHEZMEK.

Shall we go for a walk?	ghìdub bìr-àz ghèzelimmi.
I should like it much.	bàshim ùzerina èffendim.
Permit me to fetch my stick.	rùkhsatinizila bàsstunimi àlaim.
I will join you directly.	shìndi ghèlirim.
Now, I am ready to accompany you.	ìshta èffendim sìzinila ghèlmaya hàzirim.
We will go where you please.	néwàkit ìsstersiniz ghìdalim.
Which way shall we go?	hànghi yòldan ghìdalim.
Let us go into the fields.	tàrlalerin ìchindan ghìdalim.
I fear the road is dusty.	korkarim yòl pèk tòz dir.
The rain has laid the dust a little.	yàghmur bìr-àz tòzi bàsstirdi.
Let us go through the hop grounds.	hàml chìchoki "àrsassindan ghèchelim.
It is a very pleasant walk.	pèk ghyùzél ghèzejak màhàlldir.
We shall be sheltered from the sun.	ghyùncshdan hìfz olunuriz.
Will you cross this field?	bù tàrladan ghèchelimmi.
Is there a thoroughfare across this field?	bù tàrlanin ìchindan yòl chìkarmi.
Let us take this path?	bù yòli tùtalim.
It is the nearest way home.	èva an kìssa yòl bù dir.
It is not late.	ghèch dèghildir.
I want to be home in good time.	wàktila èvda bùlunmassini ìssterim.

vi sono granchiolini di mare, gam-
beri ed astachi.

a che ora volete pranzare?

pranzeremo alle sei.

il pranzo che sia pronto alle sei.

dateci macaroni e pilaf.

dateci peco pemo d'oro.

PASSEGGIARE.

anderemo a fare una passeggiata?

molto volontieri.

permettetemi di portare il mio
bastone.

sarò con voi in un memento.

sono ora pronto' a seguirla.

partiremo quando vole.

da che parte anderemo.

andiamo alla campagna.

teme che la strada è polverosa.

la pioggia ha abattuto un peco la
polvere.

traversiamo il campo dei lupoli.

è una passeggiata molto piacevole.

saremo coperti dal sole.

volete travessare questo campo?

si puó passare per mezzo di questo
campo.

prendiamo questa via.

di qui è più vicino di ritornare a
casa.

non è tardi.

deve essere nella casa in tempo.

eene karides, kaboeri ke tines
astaki.

ti oran thelete na ghevmatisite.

as gevmatisomen ees tas ex.

ees tas ex na ine etimon to ghev-
ma.

dotemis makaronia ke pilaf.

dotemis komati tomatós.

O PERIPATOS.

pighenomen na kamomen ena peri-
paton.

meta kharas.

tha sas zitiso na ipagho na paro to
rabdi moo.

ees en lepton tha eeme masi sas.

tera eeme etimos na sas akoloo-
thiso.

ipaghomen opote thelisete.

pres pion meros tha ipaghomen.

as ipaghomen ees tin exokhin.

foboome min ceme pelis konistros
to droma.

i brokhi katebalen olighon tin
skonin.

as diabomen tas brionias.

eene avtos lian evaresos peripatos.

den tha mas ke-ee o ilios.

thelete na dielthomen dia too
aghroo tootoo.

dinate tis dielthi dia tootoo too
aghroo.

as ipaghomen dia too monopatioo
tootoo.

eene sintomotatou dia na epistre-
psemen ees tin ikian.

den eene argha.

ekho diathesin na epistrepso enoris.

ENGLISH.	TURKISH.
We have only half an hour for our walk.	yòlumiz fàkat yàrim sà''āt chìkar.
We shall reach home in good time.	tāmm wàkitta èva wāssil òluriz.

CHAPTER XI.

RAIN.	YAGHMUR.
What do you think of the weather?	hàwàdān nè mèlàhéza idiyùrsiniz.
I think we shall have some rain.	zāniméh ghyùra yàghmur yàghajakdir.
I think so too, the glass falls very fast.	bènda bùylè zan idèrim zīra ghèrè ghighibi hàwa tèrāzissi àshàghilaniur.
We may have showers, for the sky is getting cloudy.	bèlki bir āz khàfīf yàghmur dushegadir chùnku hàwa bùlutlaniur.
Rain is greatly wanted.	yàghmur ziyādésile ìhtiyàjmiz vwārdér.
A little rain will do good to the gardens.	bìr-àz rāhmet bāghchalère īyi òlur.
Do you not think it very warm for the season?	mevsima ghyùra sizjè hāwa chòk sijàk dìghilmidér.
Yes; this is the warmest spring I can remember.	èvet bùndan sijàk òl bàhār hich khātirimá ghalayur.
The sun is as hot as in the middle of summer.	ghyùnèsh yàz òrtassi ghibi sìjàkdèr.
I fear we shall have cold weather after this.	kòrkarim bùndan songradé sòghuk òlajàkder.
It is very likely.	ìhtimàlder.
I have not been out since the rain.	yaghmurdanberu tàshra or dìshāri ghìtmedim.
Nor I.	bendé ghìtmedim.
Let us go and see how everything looks.	dìshārdé ālém nassil ghyùrundighini ghìdub ghyuralim.
The country looks quite different.	dìshàrissi bìtun bìtun bàshka ghyùrinyur.
It is much more pleasant walking to-day.	bù ghyùn ghèzmek dàha chòk zìyādé fèrahli dir.
The rain has laid the dust.	yàghmur tòzi bàssdirdi.

ITALIAN.	GREEK.

abbiamo mezza ora ancora di camine.

den ekhomen para imiseeas oras dromoo.

ariveremo a casa in buon tempo.

thaeemetha fthasmeni opiso enoris.

LA PIOGGIA.

EE BROKHI.

che dite di questo tempo?

tī stokhazeste peri ton kiron?

credo che pioverà.

nòmizo oti tha ekhomen brokhin.

lo credo anch' io il barometro declina molto.

k'ego nomizo ta barometron katabenī.

avrem forse qualche rovescio d'acqua perche il cielo s'oscura.

isos tha ekhomen brakhin ragdean diote o ouranos skepazete.

abbiam gran bisogna.

khrīazometha poli tin brokhin.

un pó di pioggia gioverebbe ai giardini.

olighi brokhi tha ipo kali dia ta peripolia.

non vi par egli che sia gran caldo per la stagione in che siama.

den sas fenete oti īne poli zesti analoges tis eras ton eniavton?

si, questa primavera è piu calda di tutte quelle di che mi ricordo.

nè, īne i thermotati anoiksis af'osas ego enthimosne.

il sole è tanto caldo quante nel cuor della state.

ò īlios keī os en mesete therī.

temo che dopo questo tempo non ci venga il freddo addesse.

foboome òti meta ton keron teeton tha elthi psikhra.

è da aspettarsela.

īne poli pithanon tooto.

non sono ancor uscito dope la pioggia.

den ebghika afoton epavsen i brokhi.

neppur io.

out' ego.

andiamo a vedere se tutto è fuori di bel l'aspetto.

as idomen an ta ekso ekhoon kalin opsin.

la campagna ha differente apparenza.

o kampos ekhee olos allin opsin.

oggi il camine è più agrievole.

simerou poli kallion peripatee tis.

la pioggia ha fatto cessare la polvere.

i brokhi edrosise to pan.

ENGLISH.	TURKISH.
It is not nearly so warm as it was; what a difference from yesterday!	èvvelki kàdar sìjàk dìghildir dùndan nàkadar fàrk vàr dir.
How fresh everything looks.	her bìr shèy nàkadar tāzé ghyùrinir.
The rain has revived all the plants.	ràhmet màjmà'' nèbātāti dìriltti.
A little more would do no harm.	bìr-àz dàha yàghssa zàrār ìtmaz.
How did you like your walk to-night?	bù àkhshami ghèzmeyé nassil bòldiniz.
It was delightful—very pleasant!	pèk ghyùzel ziyadésila latīf.
It is a charming evening.	pèk ghyùzel àkhshamdir.
Are you not tired?	yòrghyùnmisiniz. yòrlamadinizmi.
Not very.	chòk dìghil.
Won't you rest yourself a little?	bir āz dìnglenmezmisiniz.
No, I thank you; I shall go to bed.	khāyr tèshèkkyur ìderim yatagha ghidejaghim.
It is not late.	ghèch dèghilder.
It is time to go to bed.	yàtagha kìtmek vàktider.
I do not like to go to bed late.	yàtagha ghèch kìtmeya sevmam.
I like to go to bed in good time.	vàktindé yàtagha kìtmaghi severim.
I wish you good night.	ghèyjéniz khayr òlsun effendim.
I wish you the same.	bèndendé sùltānima khayrler òlsun.

WINTER.   KISH.

It is winter.	kìshder.
I wish the winter were over.	kyāshkè kìsh ghèchmish òlaydi.
As for me, I like winter as well as summer.	bènjé yāz vè kish mùssāvidir.
You are the only one of that opinion.	sizdan bashka ùylé zànndé kìmèssné yòkdir.
How can any one like winter?	ādem (èr) kish nassil sèvehbilur.
The days are so short and the cold is so insupportable.	ghyùnler bùylè kìssadir sòghukdé bùylé tahàmmul òlìnmāz.
One is only comfortable by the fire-side.	àtèsh yàningda òlmakjé ādem rāhat ùzāré dighildir.

ITALIAN.	GREEK.
adesso non è tanto caldo come prima, che differenza fra oggi e ieri..	den kamnee tosin zestin os pro olighoo, ti diafora tis khthesinis imeras ke simeron !
ch'aspetto di frescheza !	pos to pan eghine droseroteron.
la pioggia ha vivificato tutti i pianti.	i brokhi ezooghonisen ola ta fita.
un poco più di pioggia non forebbe male.	an ipon perissotera den tha eblapten.
come v'é paruta la passeggiata questa sera.	pos ìten ò peripatos sas apopsé.
deliziosa, molto piacevole.	ìdomicotatos, dìan evarestos.
è una bellissima sera.	ìne espera magevtiki.
non siete stanco ?	den ekoorasthité.
non molto.	okhi toson.
non volete riposarvi un poco ?	den theleté nanapavthité eligon ?
no grazie, vado a dormire.	sas evkharisto, tha ìpago na plaghiaso.
non è tardi.	den ìné arga.
è ora de coricarsi.	ìné ora ton ìpnon.
non mi piacedi caricarmi tardi.	den agape na plaghiazo arga.
mi piace caricarmi per tempo.	agape na plaghiazo enoris.
vi auguro buona notte.	sas evkhomé kalin nokta.
vi l'auguro anch' io.	k'ego episis kalon ksimeroma.

L'INVERNO.   O KHIMON.

siamo nel inverno, è inverno.	ìdon embikamen is ton khimona.
vorrei che fesse l'inverno già finite.	ìthela na īkhen ìdi parélthi o khīmona.
per me mi piace l'inverno come lo state.	ego to kat' eme agapo episis ton khīmona os ke to theres.
voi siete solo di questo opinione.	sīs īsthe mones tavtis tis gnomis.
come può piacere l'inverno ?	pos īne dinaton n' agapa tis ton khīmona.
i giorni sono corti e il freddo tanto insofferibile.	ì imerì ìne toson braksīe ke to psikhos īne toson anipoforon.
non si sta bene che al canto del fuoco.	monen plision tis thermastras evriskete tis kala.

ENGLISH.	TURKISH.
Can you skate?	bùz ùzārindé kìzàk kàya bìlirmisiniz.
Have you skated this year?	bù sèné bùz ùzārindé kìzàk kàydinizmi.
Will there be any skating to-day?	bù ghyùn bùz ùzārinda kìzàk kàymak òlajakmidir.
The ice does not bear.	hùz kàldiramaz *or* kàldirameyur.
Do you remember the hard frost?	bìr dèf''à ghàyetla kàvī bùz tùtmishdi khàtiriniza ghèliyùrmi.
Yes, it was excessively cold.	èvet effendim àshiri sòghuk ìdi.
The frost lasted two months and a half.	ìki-bùchuk àydan zìyādé hùz dàyandi.

SPRING.　ILK-BAHAR.

We have had no winter this year.	bù sèné kísh òlma di.
It is quite spring weather.	ílk-bàhār hàwasidir.
This is almost a summer's day.	bù ghyùn yàz ghyùnidir.
I have longed for spring.	ílk-bàhār ìchin chòk àrzu ìttim.
It is the season I like best.	ān sèvdikim mèvsimdir.
It is the most pleasant season.	mèvsimlerin ān fèrahlissi bùdir.
Everything in Nature smiles.	òstalikda her bù shèy tèbèssum ider ghìbidir.
Everything seems to revive.	kyāffé èshyā yèngidan, hàyāt bùliyur ghìbi ghyùruniur.
All the trees are white with bloom.	bìtun àghajler kàr yàghmish ghíbi chìchek àchdi.
If the weather prove favourable, there will be plenty of fruit this year.	ègher hàwa mùssā''id òlur ìssa bù sèné chòk yèmish òlur.
All the stone fruit has failed.	chèrkirdekli yèmishler hèp bùzuldi.
The season is very forward.	mèvsim pèk ìlèri dir.
The season is very backward.	mèvsim pèk ghèri dir.
Everything is backward.	her bìr shèy ghèridir.
Nothing is forward.	hèch bìr shèy ghèlishmadi.

ITALIAN.	GREEK.
sapete pattinare ?	īksevrete ɳa glistrate.
avete pattinato quest' anne ?	eglistrisate efetos ?
sarà qualche pattino oggi ?	tha īmporī tis simeron na glistrisi?
il ghiaccio non è abbastanza sodo.	o pages den basta.
vi ricordate del grande freddo ?	enthimīste too megalon pagon ?
si era un freddo eccessivo.	malista ìten ìperboliki psikhra.
il ghiaccio durò due mesi e mezzo.	to pages diīrkese dia īmisi minas.

LA PRIMAVERA.	TO EAR.
non abbiamo avuto inverno quest' anne.	den eekhamen kheemona to etes tooto.
è tempo di primavera.	eene esan anixis.
oggi è come giorno di state.	eene simeron esan imera kalekerioe.
desidero la primavera.	imoon ee anixis.
questa è la stagione che mi piace di più.	eene ee pothinotati mi ora too etoos.
è molto piacevole stagione.	eene ee kallisti ton oron too enavtoo.
tutto sorride nella natura.	ta panta en ti fisee ghelosi.
pare che tutte le cese rinascono.	ta panta fenonte anaghennomena.
tutti gl'alberi sono coperti di fiori.	ola ta dendra eene katalevka apo anthe.
se il tempo sarà favorevole avremo molti frutti quest' anne.	an o keros ghini kalos, tha ekhomen to etes tooto polla oporika.
tutti i frutti neccioli sono meno.	ola ta oporika pirinas den eprokopsan.
la stagione è molto inanzi.	ee ora too eniavtoo eene prokhorimeni.
la stagione è di ritardi.	ee ora too eniavtoo bradinee.
tutto è in ritardi.	ta panta bradisoosi.
niente è avansato.	tipote den eproodevse.

ENGLISH.   TURKISH.

SUMMER.   ## YAZ.

I fear we shall have a very hot summer.	kòrkarim pèk sìjàk yàz òlajakdir.
We have had no summer this year.	bù séné hìch yàz òlmadì.
We had a fire even in July.	hàttà bìz tèmmuz àyinda bìlé àtèsh yàkdik.
The meadows are mown already.	bìtun chàyrleri shìndi bìchdiler.
Hay making has begun.	kùru-òt yàpmagha bàshladiler.
There will be a great deal of hay.	chòk kùru-òt òlajak dir.
They have begun the harvest.	èkin bìchmegha bàshladiler.
The crop will be abundant.	chòk màhsūl òlajakdir.
The corn is cut already.	bòghdày shìndidan bìchdilar.
All the corn will be housed next week.	ghèlejak hàfta bòghdàyin hèpsini ìchèri àlajakler.
How hot it is!	pèk sìjàkdir.
No wonder it is so warm, we are in the dog days.	bù-kàdar sìjàk òldighina tà"àjjub ètmayelim zīra èyyāmi-bāhūr dir.

AUTUMN.   ## SONG-BAHAR.

Summer is over.	yàz bìtti.
The leaves begin to fall.	yàprakler dùkyulmagha bashliyur.
The mornings begin to be cold.	sàbāhleri sòghuk òlmogha bashliyur.
The days are much shorter.	ghyùnler pèk chòk kìssaldi.
The evenings are long.	àkhshamler ùzundir.
One cannot see at five o'clock.	sā"at bèshda "ādeta ghyùz ghyùramaz.
It is hardly light at four o'clock.	Akhsham sā"at dòrtta hàman àydinlik yòk ghìbidir.
Winter approaches.	kìsh tàkàrrub idiyur.
We shall have the shortest day in three weeks.	ùch hàftadan sòngra ān kissa ghyunda òlajakdir.
I wish it were already Christmas.	kèshké bùghyùn mèvlid hàzrèt "īssa òlayidi.
The days begin to lengthen.	ghyùnler ùzamagha bàshliyur.

ENGLISH.	TURKISH.

L'ESTATE.

temo che avremo un state molto caldo.

non abbiamo avuto state quest' anne.

abbiamo avuto fuoco ancora nel mese di Luglio.

i prati sono gia tagliati.

il fieno si cominciò ad essere tagliato.

quest' anno sarà molto fieno.

s'è cominciata la raccolta.

la raccolta sarà abbondante.

il grano è di già tagliate.

tutto il grano sarà nei granai la ·settimana veniente.

che caldo è.

non è da maravigliarsi che sia tanto caldo siamo nella canicola.

TO THEROS.

foboome mi ekhomen polla thermon to theres.

den eekhamen kalokeri tooto to etes.

anaptamen fotian akemi ke ton ioolion.

etherisan idi ta libadia.

tora kamnoon khortari.

tha een efetos poli khortari.

arkhisan ton therismon.

ee eesodia tha eene afthonos.

. eene idi therismena ghennimata.

ola ta sitira tha eene therismena tin prosekhi ebdomada.

polla thermen eene.

den eene axion thavmasmoo an ine tesi zesti, ipeedi eemetha ees ton astrismon too kines.

L'AUTUMO.

l'estate é passate.

le foglie cominciano a cadere.

le mattine cominciano ad essere freddi.

i giorni divengano di già corti.

le sere sono lunghe.

non si vede ·alle cinque.

·non è ben chiaro alle 4 di sera.

l'inverno avanza.

avremo il più corto giorno in tre settimane.

vorrei che sia già natale.

i giorni cominciano a lungharsi.

TO FTHINOPORON.

idoo parilthe to theres.

ta filla arkhizoon na piptosin.

e proiè arkhizoon na ine psikhre.

e imere arketa emikrinan.

e espere eene makre.

den fenghee pleon ees tas pente.

den fenghee ees tas tessaras oras.

o kheemon plisiazee.

entes trion ebdomadon ekhomen ta imera brakhitata.

ithela na ine idi khristooghenna.

e imere arkhizoon na meghalonoon.

ENGLISH. TURKISH.

Chapter XII.

MONEY CHANGING.	AKCHA BOZMAK.
Have you any silver?	sizda hìch ghyùmish àkcha vàrmidir.
I want change for a sovereign.	bìr àltin bòzdirmak isterim.
Can you give me change?	bàna bìr Altin bòzabilirmisiniz.
I do not think I can.	kòrkarim bòzamam.
I have no change by me.	ùzerimda bòzuk àkgham yòkdur.
I have not silver enough.	yètishajak kàdar ghyùmishim yòkdir.
Go and get it changed at the nearest shop.	àlt yàndaki dùkèn ghìt bòzdir.
I am going to try.	ghìdub bàkajaghim.
Have you changed it?	bòzdirdinmi.
Yes, here is the change.	èvvet effendim ìshta bòzuk pàra.
It is all good money!	hèpsi àyidir.
I believe so, you can try it all.	zān iderim àyidir sizda bàkiniz.
Is this shilling good?	bù bìr àyi shìlinmidir.
It does not appear good.	bù àyi ghyùrumeyur.
Let me look at it?	bàkayim.
Sound it.	yèra wùruniz.
It does not sound right.	sèssi àyi dìghildir.
I think it is bad.	zān iderim kàlpdir.
Take it back, I don't think it is good.	gheri ghyùtur zān ètmamki ayìdir.
There is much base coin about.	òrtalikda khàyli kàlp àksha vàrdir.

Chapter XIII.

DIRECTIONS ABOUT THE WAY.	YOL SORMAK BEYANINDA DIR.
Can you tell me which is the way to . . .?	kèrem idin effendim fìlanja màhàllé hànghissi yòldir.
Which is the shortest way to . .?	fìlanja yèra an kìssa yòl hànghissidir.

CAMBIO DI MONETA.

avete moneta d'argento ?

cambiatemi una lira sterlina.
potete cambiarmi una lira.

non credo che posso.
non ho moneta con me.
non ho argento abbastanza.

andate a cambiarla nella più vicina
   betega.
vade a provare.
l'avete cambiato.
si, ecce il cambio.
sono tutti buoni.
crede di si, lei puo esaminarli.

questo scillino è buono.
questo non sembra buone.
fatemi vederlo.
fatelo suonare.
non suona bene.
credo che è cattivo.
oritomatelo credo che sia cattivo.

ce ne melte menete false nella
   piazza.

ALLAGHI NOMISMATO.

ekhete arghira nomismata.

n'allaxate mian liran.
eemboreete na mi dosite nomismata dia mian liran.

den pistevo.
den ekho epano moo khalasmena.
den ekho arketon asimi.

ipaghate na t'allaxite ees to plisies-
   teron erghastirion.
ipagha na idoo.
tin allaxate.
malista, idoo.
eene ola kala.
nomiso, avnasthe de na ta exeta-
   site.
to selini tooto eene araghe kalo.
tooto den fenete kalon.
na to ido.
brontise to.
den brenta kala.
kakon to theoro.
ipaghete to opiso, den nomiso na
   ine kalon.

polla kibdila nomismata kiklofo-
   reen.

PER DOMANDARE LA VIA.

ditemi vi prego qual' è la via per
   a . . . ?
qual' è la più corta via ?

OROTESEES PERI ODOO.

tis eene, sas parakalo, ee odos dia
   na ipagho tis ees . . .
tis eene o sintomotatos dromes.

ENGLISH.	TURKISH.
Is this the way to . . . ?	filanja màhàllè bù yòlmidir.
Can you tell me whether this road leads to . . . ?	bìlirmisiniz bù yòl filan yèra chìkarmi.
Is not this the road to . . . ?	filanja màhàllé bù yòl dìghilmidir.
Am I not in the way to . . . ?	filanja yèra yòlindami ìm.
You are in the right way.	dòghru yòlinda sin.
You are not in the right way.	dòghru yòlinda dìghilsin.
You are quite out of the way.	yòlindan bìtun bìtun chìkmishsin.
Which way should I go ?	kànghi yòldan ghèdejaghim.
Go on straight before you.	dòghru ghit.
You will find a lane on your left hand.	sòl kòlunda bìr dār yòl bùlursin.
Take that lane, it will lead you to the high road.	ò yòl sizé àssl jàddéya ghètirir.
You cannot mistake your way.	yòlunizi shàshiramazsiniz.
How far is it from here ?	bùradan ùzàklighi nàkadar òlabilir.
One mile, or thereabouts.	bìr mīl yàkindir.
It may be a mile.	bìr mīl kàdar.
It is fully a league from here.	bùradan tàmām bìr sā"atlik yòldir.
It is little more than a league.	bìr sā"atlik yòldan bìr-àz ziyādé dir.
It is scarcely less than three leagues distant.	ùeh sā"atlik yòldan jùz'ī èksikdir.

INQUIRIES.   SORUSH, SU'AL ETMEK.

Do you know Mr. —, living here?	bù màhàlléda filanja effendii bìlirmisiniz.
Do you know any one of the name of . . . ?	filanja ìssimda bìr kimsé bìlirmisiniz.
I do not know any one of that name.	ùylé ìssimda kimséyi bìlmiyurim.
I believe there is.	zān iderim vàr dir.
Yes, there is some one of that name.	èvvet ò issimda bìri vàr dìr.
Do you know him ?	àni bìlirmisiniz.

ITALIAN.	GREEK.
questa è la via di . . . ?	avtos eene o dromos dia . . .
potete dirmi se questa via conduce a . . . ?	emboreete na me eepite, an o dromos ootos aghi pros . . .
non è questa la via ?	den eene odo o dromos too . . .
mi sono nella via di . . . ?	den eeme ees ton dromon too . . .
siete nella vera strada.	eesthe ees ton a lithi dromon.
non siete nella vera strada.	den eesthe ees ton a lithi dromon.
siete totalmente fuori della via.	eesthe eles exo too dromoo.
da che parte deve andare ?	pros pion meros prepee na ipagho.
vada sempre diritto.	ipaghete kat' evtheean embros sas.
troverete un vicolo a sinistra.	tha evrete ena dromaki ees t'aristera sas.
segua quel vicolo il quale vi condurrà nella strada maestra.	akoloothisate to dromaki tooto, ke tha sas ebghali ees tin meghalin edon.
non potete sbagliare la strada.	den khanete ton dromon.
quante è lontano da qui ?	posen eemboree na ine makran ap' edo.
circa, una miglia.	ee skhedon stadion.
forse sarà una miglia.	eemboree na ine en stadion.
è una buona lega.	eene mia kali levgha.
è un peco più d'una lega.	eene kati pleesteron mias levghas.
quasi meno di tree leghe.	eene skhedon trees levghe.

PER DOMANDARE. — ZITISIS.

conoscete qui il Signore . . . ?	ghnorisete edo ton Kirie ?
conoscete una persona che sichiama . . . ?	ghnorisete en prosopon onomasomenen . . .
non conosco nessuno di questo nome.	den ghnoriso kanena me tooto to onoma.
credo di si.	katikee nomiso.
si vi è una persona di questo nome.	malista eene enas tootoo too onomatos.
lo conoscete ?	ton ghnorisete ?

ENGLISH.	TURKISH.
I know him perfectly well.	àni pèk à"là bìlirim.
Can you tell me where he lives?	nèréda òturdighini bàna tà"rīf ìdabilirmisiniz.
Where does he live?	ò nèréda òturiyùr.
He lives near the fish market.	bàlik bàzārina yàkin òturur.
He lives in such a street.	fìlanja sòkakda òturur.
Is it far from here?	bùradan ùzàkmi.
It is but a very little way.	pèk àz yòldir.
Can you direct me to his house?	ànin èvina bàna sàghlik vèrabilir-misiniz.
I am going that way myself.	bèn kìndimda ò tàrafa ghìdiyurim.
I will show you where he lives.	ànin nèréda òturdighini siza ghy-ùsteririm.
I will show you his house.	èvvini siza ghyùsteririm.

CHAPTER XIV.

NEEDLEWORK.	DIKISH DIKMEK.
I want a needle.	bìr ìghné ìssterim.
What are you going to sew?	siz né dìkejàsiniz.
I am going to mend my dress.	rùbami tà"mīr ìdajaghim.
This needle is too large.	bù ìghné pèk bùyukdir.
Here is another.	ìshta bìr bàshkassi.
This is too small.	bùda pèk ùfàkdir.
Give me some thread, some silk, some cotton, some worsted.	bàna bìr-àz ìplik bìr-àz ìpèk bìr-àz tīré bìr-àz yùng ìpliki vèriniz.
What colour do you want?	né rènghda ìsstersiniz.
I want some red cotton.	kìrmizi rènghlussi ìssterim.
What is it for?	né ìsh ìchindir.
To stitch my collar.	yàkami dìkmek ìchin.
Is this the colour you want?	ìsstedighiniz rèngh bùmi dir.
This colour will not do.	bù rèngh èlvirmaz.
It is too dark.	pèk kòyudir.
It is too light.	pèk àchikdir.
It will do very well.	bù pèk à"la èlverir.
Have you finished your apron?	fūtanizi tèkmīl ìttinizmi.
Not quite.	àz kàldi.
I have had something else to do.	bàshka ìshim zùhūr ìtti.
What have you had to do?	nè ìshiniz òldi.

ITALIAN.	GREEK.
lo conosco molto bene.	ton ghnoriso poli kala.
potete dirmi dove dimera?	eexevrete na me eepite poo kati-kee?
dove dimera.	poo katikee?
dimora vicino alla pescheria.	katikee plision ees to ekhthiopo-leeon.
dimora in tale strada.	katikee ees tin deena odon.
è lontano di qui?	eene makran ap' edo?
è vicino, non è lontano.	eene pela plision.
potete dirigermi alla sua casa?	eemborite na me eepite tin ikian too?
anche io vado da quella parte.	ipagho mones presto meros ekeeno.
vi mostrerò dove dimora.	tha sas deexo poo katikee.
vi farò vedere la sua casa.	thelo sas deexee tin ikian too.

CUCIRE.	RAPTIKI.
voglie un ago.	khreeasome mian pelonin.
che cosa va cucire?	ti tha rapsete?
cucirò il mio abito.	thelo na mbaloso to forema moo.
quest' ago è molto gresso.	to peloni tooto eene para meghalon.
ecco un altro.	idoo alle.
questa è molto piccola.	tooto eene polla mikron lepton.
datemi filo di cottone di seta e di lana.	dotemi klosin, metaxi, bambaki, malli.
di che colore volete?	ti khroma thelete.
veglie cotone rosso.	thelo bombaki kokkinon.
per che cosa?	dia na kamite ti?
per cucire il mio colarino.	dia na triposo ton ghiakan moo.
queste è il colore che volete?	sas areskee avto to khroma?
questo colore non vale.	den armosee tooto to khroma.
è treppo scuro.	eene poli pathi.
è molto chiaro.	eene poli anikton.
questo è va bene.	tha teriasee poli kala.
avete finito il vostro grembiale?	eteleeosate tin podian sas?
non ancora.	okhi entelos.
ho avuto altre cese a fare.	eekha allo ti na kame.
che avete avuto a fare?	ti eekhete na kamite?

ENGLISH.	TURKISH.
I have been hemming my hand-kerchief.	chèvrémin kènārini kìvirirdim.
Then I had my gloves to mend.	àndan sòngra èldivènlerimi dìktim.
After that I darned my muslin apron.	sòngrada dùlben fūtami ùradim.
Indeed you have been very busy.	fì-'lhàkīka siz zìyādéssila mèsh-ghūl.

CHAPTER XV.

FIRE.	ATESH.
The fire is very low.	àtèsh pèk àzaliyur.
Here is a very bad fire.	bù nè àz àteshdir.
You have not kept up the fire.	àtèshi siz ghyùzetmadiniz.
You have let the fire go down.	àtèsh sùnmagha brakdiniz.
It is not quite out.	bìtun bìtun sùnmamishdir.
It must be lighted again.	tèkrār yàkmaklik lāzimdir.
Come and make up the fire.	ghèl àtèshi bìr ùydur.
What are you looking for?	né àrayursin.
I am looking for the tongs.	màshayi àrayurim.
Here they are in the corner.	ìshta kyùshédadir.
Go and fetch the bellows.	ghìt kyùruki ghètir.
Blow the fire.	àtèshi kyùruklé.
Put a few shavings on the top.	ùsstuna bìr-àz tàlash dùk.
Now put on two or three pieces of wood.	ùsstuna shíndè bìr kàch àghaj kò.
It will soon draw up.	chàbik yànār.
Are there any coals in the scuttle?	kyùmur kàbinda kyùmur vàrmi.
Take the shovel and put on some coals.	kyùrèki àlda ojagha bìr-àz kyùmur kò.
Do not put on too many at one time.	bìrdan bìra òlkader chòk kyùmur kòma.
If you put on too many coals you will put out the fire.	ègher òlkader chòk kyùmur kòrsan àtèshi sùndirirsin.
Raise them with the poker to give a little vent.	kyùsskyu ila kyùmuri kàldir bìr-àz hàwa àlsun.
Leave the poker in, and the fire will soon burn up.	kyùsskyuyi ìchinda bràk àtèsh chàbik yànar.
It will burn up presently.	shìndi pàrlar.

ITALIAN.	GREEK.
ho orlate il mio fazzoletto.	epipilosa to mandilion moo.
e poi ho cucito i miei guanti.	meta tavta eekha na rapso ta kheeroktia moo.
e poi ho rassettate il mio grambiale di mosselino.	kalopin ekama ena tsatisma ees tin apo moosoolinan podian moo.
veramente siete state molto occupato.	ti alitheea eekhete polla ergha.

FUOCO.

TO PIR.

il fuoco va smorzarsi.	i fotia eene tapeenon.
ecco un cattivo fuoco.	den eene dioloo kali avti i fotia.
non avete sustenuto il fuoco.	den esintirisate tin fotian.
avete lasciate il fuoco smorzarsi.	afisate na olighoostevsi i fotia.
non è affatto smorzato.	den esbisen olotelos.
bisogna riaccenderlo di nuovo.	prepee palin n'anapsi.
venite ed aggiustate il fuoco.	elthete na kamite tin fotian.
che cosa cercate ?	ti siteete ?
cerce le molle.	sito tin piraghran.
eccoli nella cantonata.	na tin ees tin ghonian.
andate a portare il sofietto.	ipaghate na zitisite to fisooni.
soffiate il fuoco.	psisisate tin fotian.
mettete sopra pezzi di legno.	balete ap' epano merica pelekoodia.
ora mettete due o tre pezzi di legno.	tera balete dio tria xila.
s'accenderá ben presto.	tha piasi ees mian sighmin.
v'è carbone nella secchia ?	eene karboona ees to kalathi ?
prendete la paletta e mettete carbon fossile.	parete to ftiari ke palete karboona.
non mettete molto alla volta.	mi ballete polla dia mias.
se mettete treppe carbene smerserete il fuoco.	an balete para polla tha sbisete tin fotian.
sollevatelo col tisoniere per dargli un peco d'aria.	sindavlisate tin me to sidiron, dia na pari olighon aera.
lasciate l'attizzatoio nel fuoco, e si accenderà subito.	afisate mesa to sidiron ke i fotia tha piasi oghlighora.
il fuoco s'accenderà fra peco.	tha piasi entes olighoo.

ENGLISH.	TURKISH.
It begins to blaze.	"àlevlèniyur.
Now the fire is very good.	ìshté shindi àtèsh pèk àyidir.
You have made it up very well.	pèk ghyùzel tànzīm ìttiniz.

CHAPTER XVI.

MEETING A FRIEND.	BIR DOSTA RASST GHEL-MEK.
What! are you here?	vwāy, wāy siz bùradami siniz.
You quite surprise me.	béni hàyretta bràktiniz.
I did not expect to meet you here.	bùrada sùltānima tèssāduf ètmaghi àsslā ùmut ètmadim.
I am very glad to meet you.	siza ràsst ghèldighima pik mèmnūnim.
I am very happy to see you.	effendimi ghyùrdighima pek messrūr òldim.
When did you return?	né zèmān "àvdet ìttiniz.
I came home last night.	èva dùn Akhsham ghèldim.
I came by the stage coach.	"àdi yòl "àrabassila ghèldim.
I came by rail.	dèmir yòlila ghèldim.
I came by post chaise.	mènzil "àrabassila ghèldim.
You come rather unexpectedly.	mè'mūl òlinmaksizin ghèldiniz.
Rather so.	bìr-àz ùylé dir.
I expected to remain all the summer.	bìtun yàz kàlmaghi kòrmish idim.
What makes you return so soon?	bù kàder èrken "àvdetiniza sèbeb né dir.
Some. business requires my presence here.	bà"zi kèyfìyyèt bèndénizi bùrada bùlunmaghi īj āb ìtterdi.
Hou did you like your journey?	yòldan hàz ìttinizmi.
I liked it very much.	òldikja hàz ittim.
I have had a very pleasant journey.	yòlim pèk rāhat ghèchdi.
When shall I have the pleasure of seeing you at my house?	bèndé-khānémda èffendimi nèwà-kit ghyùrabìlirim.
When will you come and dine with us?	néghyùn bèndénizda tà"ām bùyu-rursiniz.
I do not know, I have business to attend to.	bìlamem effendim zìra bìr-àz ìshlarim vàr dir.
I will try to call to-morrow.	yàrin ghèlub sizè èvda ghyùrurim.
We shall be very happy to see you.	tèshrīfinizdan pèk zìyādéssila mèmnūn òlurim.

ITALIAN.	GREEK.
comincia ad essere in fiamma.	arkhisee na kamni flogha.
adesso il fuoco è buone.	idoo tera kali fotia.
l'avete acceso molto bene.	kala tin idiorthosate.

INCONTRO D'UN AMICO.

SINAPANTISIS FILOO.

ITALIAN.	GREEK.
come! siete qui.	ti! sees edo.
mi fate davvero maravigliare.	me exafnisete eles.
non aspettavo d'incontrarvi qui.	den eperimena na sas apantiso edo.
ho molto piacere d'incontrarvi.	ekho pollin evkharistisin oti sas apanto.
ho molto piacere di vederbi.	aghalliasome oti sas blebo.
quando siete ritornato?	apo poti epestrepsate?
mi sono ritornato ieri sera.	iltha khthes to esperas.
sono venuto colla diligenza.	iltha epi tis takhiporoo amaxis.
sono venuto colla strada ferrata.	iltha me ton sidirodromon.
sono venuto cella pesta.	iltha me to takhidromeeon.
siete venuto all' improviso.	erkheste aprosdokitos.
si, un poco.	ne, olighon.
credevo di restarmi tutto lo state.	estokhasomin na meeno ekec elon to theres.
perche siete ritornato cosi presto?	ti sas ekame na epistrepsete toson takheos.
alcuni affari chiedono la mia pre-senza qui.	ipothesees tines apetoon tin edo paroosian moo.
come vi piaqui il vostro viaggio?	pos sas efani to taxeedion sas.
mi piaque molto.	poli evkhariston.
ho avuto un viaggio dilettevole.	ito to taxeedion moo poli evareston.
quando avrò il piacere di vedervi a casa mia?	pote tha ekho tin evkharistisin na sas ido ees tin ikian moo.
quando venirete a pranzare con noi?	pote thelete na elthete na singhev-matisomen.
non lo so, ho alcuni affari da finire.	den eexevro, ekho tinas ipothesees na teleeoso.
verrò a vedervi domain.	eltho na sas ido avrion.
avremmo molto piacere di vedervi.	tha evkharistithomen lian an sas idomen.

CHAPTER XVII.

GARDEN. FRUIT.   YEMISH.

Will you come and take a turn in the garden ?	bāghchayi bìr dèvr ètmek ìsstermisiniz.
With pleasure.	mèmnūn òlurim.
I am very fond of a garden.	bāghchadan ghāyetla hàzz ìderim.
There is a fine show of plums this year.	bù séné èrik bèrékèti ghyùsstèriyur.
The plums begin to set.	èrikler bàghlamagha bàshliyur.
They are already set.	tùtmishlar dir.
How thickly they hang.	nàkadar sìk dùruyurler.
They are much too thick.	zìyādéssila sikidir.
They want thinning.	sèyreltmek ìsster.
There will be very few apricots this year.	bù sèné pèk àz kàysi òlur.
They have generally failed.	èksérìyyā bòzuldiler.
How tempting the peaches look.	bù shèftāliler ìnsānin àghzini sùlandirir.
You have plenty of nectarines.	tùysiz shèftāliniz chòkdir.
The tree bears a great many every year.	bù àghach her séné chòk vèrir.
This tree is a great bearer.	bù àghachin chòk màhsūli òlur.
Cherries and strawberries are now in their prime.	kìrāz vè chìlèyk shìmdi kèmālda dir.
They will soon be ever.	shimdì chàbik ghètcherler.
These grapes are quite ripe.	bù ùzumler pèk à"la òlmishlar.
I had some ripe a week ago.	bìr hàfta èvvel bànda òlmishi vàr ìdi.
They are very early.	pèk èrkendir.
This vine has a fine aspect.	bù àssma ghyùnèsha kàrshi dìkilmishdir.
How are the trees in your orchard?	bāghnizdaki àghachler nàssldir.
They are loaded with fruit.	ànlar mèyvè dòli dir.

FLOWERS.   CHICHEK.

You have not seen my flowers.	chìcheklerimi ghyùrmadiniz.
Come and see my roses.	ghèl ghyùlerimi ghyùriniz.

FRUTTI.

volete fare un giro nel giardino ?

volentieri.
il giardino mi piace molto.
i susini promettino molto quest'
anno.
le susine comminciano a formassi.
sono di gia formati.
come sono suspesi pieni ;
sono molto pieni.
hanno bisogna d'essere più legieri.
sarà peco apricotto quest' anne.

sono generalmente mancati.
che bel celere hanno queste
pesche!
avete molto brugnoni.
quest' albero da gran quantità
ogni anno.
quest' albero produce melta frutta.

le ciriegie ed i frauli sono adesso
in stagione.
fra peco saranno passati.
queste uve sono maturi.
ho avuto alcuni maturi una settimana fà.
sono molto avanti il tempo.
questa vigna è in una buona
posizione.
come sono i alberi nel vostro orte?

sono pieni di frutta.

FIORI.

non avete veduto i miei fiori.
venite a vedere le mie rose.

E OPORE.

thelite na kamite ena ghiron ees
ton kipen ?
meta kharas.
aghapo poli too kipen.
e damaskinee iposkhonte polin
karpen tooto to etes.
ta damaskina arkhiroon na denoon.
ederan idi.
posen megha poson avton !
eene para poli pikna.
eene khria na areothon.
tha ghinoon polla oligha perikokka
efetos.
en ghenee den eprokopsan.
ti kalin theorian ekhoon tavta ta
rodakina.
ekhete polla rodakina.
to dendron tooto didee meghalin
posotita kata pan etes.
tooto to dendron karpoforee me-
ghalos.
ta karasia ke ta khamokerasa eene
tora ees ton keron ton.
th'aperasoon met'olighon.
to stafili tooto eene en telos orimon.
ekha egho orimon stafili pro okto
imeron.
eene pro-eron poli.
to klima tooto eene ees kalin
thesin.
pos eene ta dendra ees ton den-
drena sas.
eene fortomena apo karpon.

TA ANTHI.

den eedete ta anthi moo.
telhete na idite triandafili moo.

ENGLISH.	TURKISH.
They are beautiful!	ànlar pèk ghyùzèldir.
How quickly the flowers come up.	chìchekler chàbik sùriyur.
The crocuses have been some time in bloom.	khàyli vàkitdir chīghdim chìchek-dadir.
The daffodils will soon come out.	àltin-tòp yàkinda àchar.
Are your tulips open?	sìzin lāléleriniz àchtimi.
Yes. We shall see them presently.	èvvét effendim, shindi ànlari ghyù-rajaghiz.
What a fine bed of them you have.	àmān effendim bù tàrhda nàkadar chòkdir.
The hyacinths are almost over.	sùnbullerin wàkti hàman ghètchi-yur.
What flower is this?	bù né chìchekdir.
What is the name of this flower?	bù chìcheghin àdi né dir.
What a beautiful double wall-flower!	né ghyùzèl bìr kàtmèr sàrishèb-bùydir.
Here is a fine double stock.	né ghyùzél bìr kàtmèr kìrmizi sàrishèbbùydir.
Yes, but I do not like the scent.	evvèt effendim lākin kòkussin-danhàz ètmam.
You have not seen my jessamine.	yàsséminlerimi ghyùrmadiniz.
You have a very fine collection of flowers.	pèk ìlérida chìchekleriniz vàr dir.
You keep your garden very neat.	bàghchanizi zìadassila tèmīz tòti-yùrsiniz.
Your garden is kept in perfect order.	bàghchanizi nìzāmi "àla ālā"la dir.

VEGETABLES.

. ZERZEWAT.

Now I must pay a visit to your kitchen garden.	shimdi èffendim zèrzéwāt bàgh-chanizi zìyārèt ètmaliim.
How everything grows!	hèr bìr shèy nàssl à"la bìyùmakda dir.
The rain has done much good.	rahmet chòk àyi ètti.
We wanted it greatly.	yàghmura pèk mùhtāj ìdik.
What a quantity of cabbages and cauliflowers.	né chòk làhana vè kàrnabit vàr.
Here is a fine bed of asparagus.	ìshta pèk ghyùzèl kùsh-kònmàz tàkhtassi.
I like it much.	ànlari pèk chòk sèverim.

ITALIAN.	GREEK.
sono belissimi.	eene oreotata.
i fiori crescono ben presto.	ta anthi fenonte afthona.
i zafferani sono già fioriti.	eene idi oligho keros afotto erkhise n' anthisi o krokos.
i narsisi·fra poco fioriranno.	i narkissi tha anthisoon takheos.
i vostri tulipani sono fioriti ?	anthisan ta toolipania sas.
si, adesso li vedremo.	malista, tha tas idomen met' olighon.
che bellissima aiola avete !	ti lambra prosian ekhete avton !
i giacinti sono quasi passati.	i iakinthi skhedon eperasan.
che fiore è questo ?	ti anthos eene tooto edo.
come sichiama questo fiori ?	pos onomasete tooto to anthos.
che bel ravenelli dopii !	ti orea biola dipli.
ecce un bel girofiori dopio.	idoo mia orea dipli gharoofalia.
si, ma non mi piace l'edere.	ke, alla den aghapo tin mirodian ton.
non avete veduto i miei giassimini.	den eedete iasimine moo.
avete una bella collezione di fiori.	ekhete axiologhon silloghin anthen.
voi tenete il vostro giardino molto polito.	krateete lian katharon ton kipen sas.
il vostro giardino è in perfetta ordine.	o kipos sas diatireete arista.

LEGUMI.

LAKHANIKA.

vade a fare una visita al vostro giardino.	tora thelo na kame mian episkepsiu is ton lakhanokipon sas.
come le cese crescino !	pos ta panta blazanoon.
la pioggia ha giovato molto.	i brokhi ofelise poli.
l'avevamo molto bisogno.	eekhamen to·enti ananghin avtis.
che quantità di cavoli e di cavoli-fiori.	posi posotis krambis ke antha-krambis.
che bella piantata di sparagi.	idoo mia kalà fiteea asparaghon.
mi piacino molto.	egho ta aghapo iperballontos.

ENGLISH.	TURKISH.
I like artichokes nearly as well.	ìnghinārida hàman àular kàder sèverim.
These pears are already in bloom.	bù bèzèlyalar shìndidan chìcheklenmishdir.
I have some in pod elsewhere.	dígher bìr màhàllda kàbuk bàghlanmishi dè vàr dir.
Have you planted any kidney beans?	hìch fàssūlya ìkdinizmi.
I have some up.	bìr-àz sùrmishi vàr dir.
You will have them very early.	bà"zissi khàyli èrken òlajàdir.
Here are French beans in blossom.	ishta chìcheklinmish bàkla.
You will have a good crop.	chòk bàklaniz òlajàkdir.
What is this?	bù né dir.
It is salsify.	ùsskurchana dir.
Further on are carrots and parsnips.	ùzakdakida hāwuj vè yàban hāwuj.
What have you there?	òradaki né dir.
Those are Jerusalem artichokes.	yèr èlmassidir.
I had not seen any before.	àslan "ùmrèm ichinda ghyùrmadim.
Are these onions?	bùnlar sòghanmidir.
No. They are leeks.	khàyr, pràssadir.
They are very much like onions.	sòghana chòk bèngzer.
I see you have all kinds of salad.	sizda her tùrlu sàlata vàr ghyùriyurim.
Here are cabbage lettuce and goss lettuce.	ìshta tòp sàlata vè mārul.
This is endive.	ìshta fìrènk sàlatassi.
I prefer it to lettuce.	àni mārula tàrjīh iderim.
You have a good supply.	àndan sìzda pèk chòk vàr dir.
I do not see any celery.	hìch kèréviz ghyùramiyurim.
It is in another part of the garden.	bàghchanin bàshka bìr tàrafindadir.
I think your garden is well stocked.	sizin baghchanìz hèr bìr shèy iladòludir.
You have plenty of everything.	sizdé hèr bìr shèy zìadéssila mèvjùddir.
It is better to have too much than too little.	àz òlmadan issa chòk òlmassi ūlà dir.

ITALIAN.	GREEK.
i carcioffoli mi piacino anche.	egho aghapo skhedon episis tas anghinaras.
questi piselli sono gia fioriti.	ta pizellia avta eene idi ees to anthoston.
ne ho alcuni in bacelli in altre luoge.	ekho alloo me leboes idi.
avete piantato favoli?	efitevsate fasoolia?
ne ho alcuni già sopra terra.	ekho tina avton idi ekblastisanta.
avrete alcuni di bon ora.	tha ta ekhete enkeros.
ecco le fasulie sono in fiori.	idoo kookkia anthoonta.
avrete una grande ricolta.	tha ekhete avton pallin ees sodian.
che cosa é questo?	ti eene tooto.
sono salsofie.	eene traghopoghon.
più in avanti sono carete e pastinache.	parakee eene davkia ke kolokasia.
che cosa avete là?	ti ekhete ekee.
sono tartufi bianchi.	eene enkenares tis ieroosalim.
non ho mai veduto prima.	den eekha idin pete moo eos tera.
sono cipolle questi?	avta edo krommidia eene.
no, sono prasa.	okhi, eene prasa.
rassimigliano ai cipolle.	omiasoon poli ta krommidia.
vedo che avete molte specie di salata.	blebo oti ekhete pan cedes salatas.
ecce di latuga.edi capocci.	idoo ghalaxidan ke marooli.
questa è cicoria.	tooto eene kikhorion.
mi piace più della lattuga.	to protimo para tin ghalaxida.
avete abbondanza di loro.	ekhete lipen avto arthonon.
non vedo alcun sedano.	den blebo dioloo selina.
è in un altra parte del giardino.	ekeena eene ees alle meros too kipoo.
mi pare che il vostro giardino è ben piene.	o kipes sas mi fenete arketa kala pepliromenos.
avete abbondanza di tutte.	ekhete polla apo kathe cedes.
è meglio d'avere troppo che d'avere peco.	kallion na ekhi tis polla para oligha.

CHAPTER XVIII.

GOING TO SCHOOL.	MEKTEBA GHITMEK.
Where are you running so fast?	bù sùr "àtla nèreya kòshiyursiniz.
I am going to school, did you not hear the bell?	mèkteba ghìdiyurim changhi ìshìt-madinizmi.
Certainly I did, but why should we hurry, we shall be there in time.	èlbètté ìshìttim lākin nichin kéndimizi yòrulayim òrada wàkitta bùluniriz.
We have plenty of time, the bell has only just ceased ringing.	wàktimiz chòkdir changhin sèssi kèssildi bìr dàkika ghèchmadi.
See—there are a great many boys still behind.	bàk àrkamizda dàha nàkadar chòkler var.
Let us wait for them, we will go in together.	ànleri bèkleyalim jùmlé miz bìrdan ìcheri ghìdalim.
If you like to come with me, we will run; if not, good-bye.	ègher bènimlè ghèlmeghi isstersaniz kòshalim ègher ghèlmeyissaniz àllāha ìssmàrladik.
For my part, I will not remain another moment.	ègher bènge sòrarsiniz bìr dakika dàha bèklayamam.

LETTER WRITING.	MEKTUB YAZMAK.
What are you looking for?	nè àrayursiniz.
I am looking for a steel pen.	bìr dèmir kàlem bàkayurim.
Here are several.	ishta bùrada bìr khàli vàr.
Thank you, I will take this.	tèshèkkyur iderim bùni àlerim.
Will you kindly lend me a pen holder?	bìr kàlem sàpi ùdunj ìshsān idiniz.
This is a bad pen, it cuts the paper.	bù kàlem pèk fànadir kyāghidi kèssiyur.
Choose another.	dígherini intikhāb idiniz.
Can you lend me a sheet of paper?	bàna bìr tàbaka kyāghid ùdunj vèrirmisiniz.
What sort of paper do you want?	nassl kyāghid isstersiniz.
Some note paper, I have not a single sheet in my desk.	bìr-àz mèktubi kyāghidi hàttà bìr tàbaka bìlé chèkméjémda yòkdir.
Here is one. If it is not enough, I have more at your service.	ìshta bìr tàbaka ègher kyāfi dighilissa banda daha vàr ìstayeniz effendim.

ANDANDO A SCUOLA.

dove correte tanto presto ?
vade alla scuola, non avete inteso la campanella ?
certamente, ma perche tanta frettura ? arriveremo in tempo.

ancora abbiamo tempo, la campana si fermò un minuto fà.
vedete quanti scolari sono dietro di noi.
aspettiamoli affinche intreremo insieme.
se volete venire con me, corriamo, altrimenti, addie.

io non fermerò un memento di più.

TO ESKOLEEON FITISIN.

poo trekhete tose spoodeos.
ipagho is ton skoleeon den ikoosate too skoleeoo ton kodona.
anamribolos, alla tis i ananki na spevdomen, tha fthasomen arketa enkeros.

ekhomen da keron. molis ipavsen apo too na simeni o kedon.
idete, posi akemi mathite erkhonte katopin imon.
as toos perimeenomen, ke embenemen oli omoo.
an thelete na elthite mazi moo, trekhomen, ee de mi, ighiene.

to kat'ame den meno oode stighmin.

SCRIVERE LETTERE.

che cercate ?
cerco una penna d'acciaio.
eccone molti.
vi ringrazio prenderò questa.
mi fa piacere di prestarmi un porta penna.
questa penna è cattiva, taglia la carta.
scheglietevi un altra.
potete prestarmi un foglio di carta ?
che specie di carta volete ?
carta di lettere, non ho ne pure un foglio nella cassetta.

ecce uno, se queste non è pastanza ne ho ancora al vostro servizio.

GHRAPSE EPISTOLIN.

ti ziteete.
zito kondilion metallinon.
idoo polla.
sas evkharisto. tha paso tooto.
parakalo dote mi ena kondiloforon.

to kondilion tooto ine kakon, eskhizeeto kharti.
dialexete alle.
dinasthe na me danessite fillon khartoo.
ti cedos khartoo thelete.
khartin di' epistolas, den ekho tiootoo khartioo oode en fillon ees tin thikin moo.

labe en fillon, an den sas arki en ekho ke alle ees tin diathesin sas.

ENGLISH.	TURKISH.
Many thanks, one sheet will do.	effendima tèshèkkyurler iderim lākin bìr tàbaka yètishir.
I will return it to you later, for I am going to send for some.	àni bìr-àzdan siza ghèri vèrerim chùnku bìr-àz ìssmàrlamaya ghidiyurim.
There is no hurry. But tell me, to whom are you going to write?	"àjéléssi yòkdir, lākin effendim, kima mèktub yàzajaksiniz.
I am going to write to my people.	dòsstlerima yàzajaghim.
I thought so. Present my compliments to them.	bèndenizdé ùylé zān ittim, bandan, sàlām sèyleniz.
I will, without fail.	bàshim ùsstuma, ùnùtmam.
Can you lend me your penknife?	chàkinizi bàna bir àzijik vèra bilirmisiniz.
Will you have the goodness to lend me your penknife?	kèrem ìdub chàkinizi bàna bìr-àz vèrermisiniz.
What do you want it for?	né ichin ìsstersiniz.
I want to make a pen.	bìr kàlem yòutmak ìchin issterim.
I prefer a quill.	tùy kàlemi tèrjīh iderim.
My pen is good for nothing.	kàlemi hìch bìr ìsha yàramaz.
It wants mending.	dùzèltmek ìssterim.
Why do you not use your own knife?	kèndi chàkinizi nichin kùllanme-yursiniz.
It does not cut.	kèssmeyur.
It is blunt.	kyùr dir.
It wants setting.	bìlenmèk isster.
I cannot use mine.	bènimkini kùllanamam.
It is entirely spoilt.	bìtun bìtun bòzulmishdir.
Shall I make your pen for you?	sizin ìchin kàleminizi àchayimmi₁
Thank you much.	tèshèkkyur iderim.
If it is not too much trouble.	ègher sizleré chòk zàhmet òlmaz issa.
Will you have it hard or soft?	sèrtmi yòkhsa yimùshàkmi isster₁ siniz.
Here it is. Try it.	ìshta effendim tèjribé idiniz.

ITALIAN.	GREEK.
mille grazie, un foglio basterà.	sas evkharisto, en fillon th' arkesee.
vi restituirò fra peco, perche vado a comprare alcuni.	sas to apodido parevthis, dioti tera stello n' aghoraso.
non ce premura, ma dite a chi scrivete?	oodemia bia, all'eepate mi ees pion. mellete na ghrapsite.
sto a scrivere alla mia famiglia.	tha ghrapso ees tin ikogheneean moo.
lo pensava, presentategli i miei complimenti.	to ipetheta, prosferete ke ta ema sebasmata.
non scorderó.	den tha, leepso.
potete prestarmi il vostro temperino.	mi daneezate to kondilomakheron sas.
volete avere la compiacenza di prestarmi il vostro temperino.	labete parakalo tin klosinin na mi danessite to kondilomakheron sas.
perche cosa la volete?	dia na kamete ti.
veglio temperare una penna.	ithela na kamo en kondilion.
preferisco una penna di piume.	protimo khinision kondilion.
la mia penna non vale niente.	to kondilion moo den axeesee tipoti.
ha bisogna d'essere temperata di nuovo.	eene khria na xanafkiasthi.
perche non usate il vostro temperine?	dia ti den metakhresesthe to kondilomakheron sas.
non taglia.	den koptee.
è spuntata.	eene ambli.
ha bisogna d'essere aguzzate.	prepee na trokhisthi.
non posso servirmi del mio.	den tha idinamin na metakheeristho to edikon moo.
è totalmente rovinato.	eene eles dioloo khalasmenon.
volete che temperirò la vestra penna?	thelete na sas kamo to kondilion sas.
molte grazie.	tha sas evkharisto.
se non vi do molto incomodo.	an den sas ine okhliron.
volete che sia dura o molle?	thelete na ine skliron i malakon.
eccola, provatela.	idoo avto dokimasate to.

ENGLISH.	TURKISH.
How do you like it?	nàssl bèghendiniz.
The slit is rather too long.	bìr-àz chàkja yàralmishdir.
I am very much obliged to you.	sizlera chòk tèshèkkurler iderim.
I am going to fold my letter.	mèktubimi bùkyùjaghim.
Give me an envelope.	bàna bìr mèktub zàrfi vèriniz.
Now I have only the address to write.	shìndi fàkat mèktubin usstini yàzajaghim.
The letter is not sealed.	mèktub mùhurlanmamishdir.
There is no sealing wax.	bàlmùmu yòkdir.
Bring me a wafer.	bàna bìr mèktub pùli ghètir.
Where is my seal?	mùhrum nèradadir.
Take this letter to the post office.	bù mèktubi pòsta khanaya ghìtir.
Pay the postage.	pòsta pàrassini vèr.

Chapter XIX.

RISING.	· YATAKDAN KALKMAK.
Who is there?	kìmdir ò.
It is I, get up.	bèn im, kàlkiniz.
What o'clock is it?	sā"at kàchdir.
It is time to get up.	kàlkmak wàktidir.
Already! Impossible, I have not been in bed two hours.	shìndi mi, mùmkin dìghildir dàha yàtagba ghirdighim ìki sā"at.
I was so comfortable when you awoke me.	beni òykudan òyandirdikiniz wàket né kàdar ràhāt idim.
Indeed, it is a great pity.	ghèrchèkmi né yàzikdir.
Make haste, and dress quickly.	chàbik òl rùbanizi ghìyiniz.
Why such a hurry?	"àjèlè nédir.
All the boys have been in school a quarter of an hour or more.	chòjuklerin hèppssi mèkteba ghìttighi bìr chèyrekdan ziadedir.
Well, can they not begin without me?	èy, né, bènsiz dèrsslerina bàshlayameyurlarmi.
Come, I have no time to argue with you.	ghèl, ghèl, seninla mū"āraza ètmagha wàktim yòkdir.
Make haste I say, and come down at once.	chàbik òl sàna diyurim hamān ashagha ghèl.

ITALIAN.	GREEK.
come vi piace ?	pos sas fenete.
è troppo aperta.	eene para skhismenon.
sono molte obligato.	sas eeme lian ipokhrios.
vado fermare la mia lettera.	idi diplono tin epistolin moo.
datemi un anviloppo.	dote mi en periteelima.
non ho altre che l'indirizzo di scrivere.	tora den mi menee para na ghrapso tin epinghrafin.
la lettera non è sigillata.	i epistoli den eene esfraghismeni.
non cè di cera.	den ekhomen boollokeri.
portatemi una estia.	ferete mi mian ostian.
deve è il mio sigillo ?	pete sfraghsis moo.
portate questa lettera alla posta.	ipaghete to ghramma tooto ees to takhidromeeon.
francatela.	proplirosate to.

LEVARE. ALSARE.	EGHERSIS.
chi è là ?	tis ee.
son io, levatevi.	egho eene, zikoo.
che ora é ?	ti ora eene.
e tempo di levarsi.	eene ora egerseos.
già! è impossibile, non sono ancora due ore di poi che mi son dormito.	idi! adonaton, den eene dio ore afotoo eplaghiasa.
stava tanto bene quando m'avete svegliato.	anepavomin toson kala, ote m' exipnisate.
è molto peccato, sicuramente!	krima to-onti.
fate presto vestite.	alla kamet' eghrighora ke endithete.
perche tanta premura ?	ke eene kammia bia.
tutti i ragazzi sono di già nella scuola più d'un quarto d'ora.	parilthen idi tetarton tis ora af'otoo oli i mathite eene ees tin paradosin.
ebbene non possono comminciare senza di me ?	ke ti den imboroon n'arkhisoon khoris eme.
orsù! non ho tempo di disputare con voi.	ela! den ekho keron na loghotribo mazi sas.
fa presto e scendete subito.	spevsate, sas legho, ke katabite ameses.

ENGLISH.   TURKISH.

Chapter XX.

TRAVEL TALK.   YOL SUHBETDIR.

Sir, are you from Turkey?   effendim siz dèvléti "àlìyyénin tàba"asimisiniz.

Yes, Sir, I am.   èvvet effendim.

From what part of Turkey do you come?   tùrkianin né tàrafindan siniz.

From Stamboul, from Damascus.   stambuldan, shām èyâlètindan.

Have you been long in England?   ìnghilterrada chòktamisiniz.

About ten years.   òn sènédir.

You are almost naturalized.   siz hàman bitùn bitùu ìnghiliz òlmush siniz.

How do you like England?   inghilterrayé nàssl sèviyursiniz.

I like it very much.   chòk sèverim.

You like Turkey better, do you not?   turkia dàha ziyāde sèversiniz dighilmi.

True, one cannot help preferring his own country.   sàhīhdir effendim zira bìr àdam kendi mèmlekctini tèrjīh ider.

I do not blame you, it is natural.   sìzi tà"yīb ètmam zira tàbī"ī dir.

Is it true that it is warmer there in summer, and colder in winter than here?   sàhīhmídirki yāz òrada bùradan sìjàkdir vè kìsh sòghukjadir.

Our summers are both longer and hotter, but the winters not so severe as here.   bìzim yàzimiz hèm ùzundir vè hèmda sijakdir vè kìshimizda bùradan shìddètlidir.

Sir, you know where I live?   effendim bènim nèrada òturdughimì bilirsiniz.

I shall always be glad to see you when you like to call.   né wàkit bèndanizi ghyurmagha tèshrīf bùyurirsaniz hèr dā'im mànun òlurim.

You are very kind, but I am afraid of intruding.   effendim mùrùvvèt bùyurirsaniz lākin sizlara zàhmet òlmakdan khàwf iderim.

Do not fear that, I like Easterns, and it is always a pleasure to see them in my house.   kòrkma bèn shàrkilari sèverim wè èvimda ànlari ghyurmekdan dā'imé hàzz iderim.

I will do myself the honour now and then.   àra sìrà effendimi zìyārètla mùshèrrèf òlurim.

CONVERSAZIONE NEL VIAGGIO.

Signore è dalla Turchia?

si Signore io sono.
di che parte della Turchia voi siete?
da Costantinopoli, da Damasco.

siete da molte tempo in Inghilterra?
circa dieci anni.
è quasi naturalizzato.

come vi piace l'Inghilterra?
mi piace molto.
amate la Turchia meglio non è vero.
è vero signore, ma ciascuno preferisce la sua patria.
non vi biasimo e cosa naturale.
è vero che nella state è più caldo e nell' inverne più freddo di qui?
i nostri stati sono più lunghi e più caldi ed i nostri inverni più freddi di qui.
signore sapete dove resto.

avrò sempre piacere di vedervi quando vorra venire a vedermi.

voi siete molto gentile ma temo d'incommodarvi.

non avete paura, amo i orientali e ho sempre gran piacere di vedergli nella mia casa.

mi farò l'enore di venire alcuni volte.

OMILINE EN TAXEEDION.

eesthe, Kirie apo Anatolia.

malista Kirie.
apo pion meros tis Turkias eesthe.

apo tin Stimbolin, apo tin Damaskion.

eene keros afotoo eesthe en Anghlia.
eene deka eti.
liben skhedon eghinete entopios.

pos sas fenete i Anghlia.
aghapo polla.
aghapate i Turkia kallion den ine.

eene alithes, Kirie, alla dinate tis na mi protima tin patrida too.
den sas memfome fisikon tooto.
eene alithinon oti ekee eene pleeotera zesthi to theros ke pleeotera psikhra ton khimona pares edo.
ta kalokeria par' imin eene makrotera ke thermotera ke i khimones mas eene dremiteri ton edo.
Kirie, exevrete poo katiko.

asmenestata tha sas blepo osakis thelisete na metimisite.

eesthe, Kirie, peripi-itikotatos, all' egho foboome mi sas enokhliso.

mi fobisthe, egho aghapo toos anatolikoos ke pantote me eene evkharistisis na toos dekhome en ti ikia moo.
tha lambano lipen tavtin ti timin apo keroo ees keron.

CHAPTER XXI.

IN A SHOP.	DUKENDA.
Have you any fine cloth?	àyi chòkaniz vàrmi.
What sort of cloth do you wish for?	né tùrlu chòka isstersiniz.
To what price do you wish to go?	né pàhaya kàdr òlsun.
We have some of all prices.	bizda hèr bìr pàhada chòka var.
Show me the best you have.	èn à''làsindan ghyùster.
Is this the finest?	en ìnja chòkaniz bù mi dir.
Here is some good cloth for summer wear.	yàz ìchin ìshta bù à''la chòkadir.
If it is for trousers, I recommend this cloth.	ègher pàntalòn ìchin issa siza bù chòkayé nàssīhàt idèrim.
I advise you to take that cloth.	sizin òl chòkayi àlmanizi nassīhàt iderim.
I warrant it strong.	kàvi òldighini sùz vèrerim.
I have just enough left to make a coat.	àndan bènda tàmām bìr sètrilik kàldi.
This will make you a splendid cloak.	bù siza bìr à''la kàpud òlur.
At how much do you sell it per yard?	àrshinina né isstersiniz.
The price is twenty shillings a yard.	àrshinini yìghirmi shillina sàti-yurim.
It is very expensive.	chòk pàhallidir.
What is the lowest price, for I do not like to bargain?	èn àshaghi kàcha òlur sira pàzar-lashmakdan hazz itmam.
Sir, I never ask more than I mean to take.	effendim bèn àlajaghimdan zìyada àssla isstamam.
I have only one price.	bèn yàlaniz bìr pàha sewyelerim.
Can you let me have it for . . . ?	fìlan pàhaya vèrermisiniz.
I cannot take less.	mùmkin dìghil àshàghi vèramam.
You know I am a good customer.	bilirsiniz bèn dā'imā bìr mùshtérī ìm.
Do yo wish for anything else?	bìr shèy dàha isstermisiniz.
Let me see your patterns.	ùrneklerini ghyùraim.
I want some material for a waistcoat.	yèlek ichin bìr-àz kùmāsh issterim.
Do you like white?	bèyāz sèvermisiniz.

IN UN MAGAZZINO.	EN ERGHASTIRIO.
avete panno fino?	ekhete kalin tsokhan.
che sorte di panno desiderate?	ti eedos tsokhas epithimeete.
a che prezzo lo vuolete?	ti timin ithelete desee.
abbiamo di tutti i prezzi.	ekhomen pasin timis.
mostratemi il migliore che avete.	deexate mi oti ekhete kallisten.
questo è il più fino?	avti eene i kalitera ton oson ekhete.
ecce bon panno per uso di state.	idoo kali tsekha dia to kalokeri.
se lo vuolete per calzoni vi raccommando questo panno.	an ine dia pantalonia sas sisteno avtin tin tsokhan.
vi consiglio di prendere questo.	sas simboolevo na parete avtin tin tsokhan.
vi garantisco che é forte.	sas tin enghiome.
è rimaste abbastanza per fare un surtu.	me menee perissevma apo avtin tin tsokhan oson dia mian beladan.
queste vi farà un bel mantello.	apo avto kamnete ena exereton mandian.
per quante vendete la jarda.	posen poleete to metron.
il prezzo è venti scillini per la jarda.	i timi eekosi selinia to metron.
è molto caro.	eene poli akribon.
ditemi l'ultimo prezzo perche non mi piace di contratare.	pia eene i televtea sas timi, epeedi den aghapo na praghmatevome.
Signore, io non demando più di quele che vuoglio prendere.	den legho, Kirie, pete iperbolikin timin.
ne ho un prezzo solamente.	den ekho para mian monin timin.
potete darmila per . . . ?	dinasthe na mi tin dosite dia . . .
non posso prendere di meno.	den eemboro na labo olighoteron.
sapete che sono un buon aventore.	ixevrete oti eeme kalos thamonis (moosteris).
desiderate qualche altra cosa?	epithimeete akomi ke allo ti.
mostratemi le vestre mostre.	deexate mi ta deeghmata sas.
vuoglio una stoffa per fare un gilè.	khreeazome ifasma dia ghelekion.
vi piace il bianco?	aghapate levkon.

ENGLISH.	TURKISH.
This kerseymere is good.	bù kàzmir ghyùzèl dir.
This colour is too dull.	bù rènk pèk dùnuk dir.
That is too light.	bù pèk àchikdir.
I want something which will not soil quickly.	kìr ghìtirir bìr shèy issterim.
I want a washing material.	yìkanabilir bir shèy issterim.
Is this a fast colour?	bùnun bòyassi àyimidir.
I like this pattern very well, but fear the colour is not fast.	ìshta bù rènkdan òldukja bàzz iderim làkin kòrkarim rènghi sùlar.
I am afraid this material will not wear well.	kòrkarim bù kùmāsh chòk dàyànmaz.
On the contrary, it is excellent.	khàyr effendim "àkssina sùwèyliyursiniz.
You will never wear it out.	èsskitmazsiniz.
You may take it on my word.	bàna inànub àni àliniz.
Now let me know what I owe you.	shìndi siza né bòrjìm vàr sùwèylaniz.
What does it come to?	nàkadar dir.
Here is your account.	ishta hèssapiniz.
It comes in all to seventy-two francs.	mèjmū"i yètmish iki franka bāligh.
Are you not mistaken?	yānishiniz yòkmidir.
The account is right, you can add it up.	yèghyūni dòghridir sizda hèssap idiniz.
Here are four Napoleons, which make eighty francs, you can give me the change.	ìshta siza dùrt altin sèksèn frank ider siz bana kùssūri vèriniz.
Here it is, Sir.	ìshta effendim.
Send that at once.	bùni dèr-"àkab bàna ghyùnder.
You shall have it in ten minutes.	òn dàkīka zàrfinda ìrsāl iderim.

CHAPTER XXII.

BOOKSELLER.	KITABJI ILA.
You have lately received an assortment of French books, I should like to see them.	ghèchinlerda bìr khàyli firansizja kìtābler àlmìshdiniz ànlari ghyùrmek isterim.

ITALIAN.	GREEK.
questo cascimir è buone.	to kazimiri tooto eene kalon.
questo colore è troppo escuro.	to khroma tooto eene para skotinon.
questo è molto chiaro.	tooto den eene para anikton.
veglie qualche cosa che non si sporca presto.	thelo ti to opien na mi eeroni evkola.
veglio qualche cosa che si lava.	thelo ti to opien na plinete.
questo colore è fermo ?	tooto to khroma eene ara ghe kalos bammenon.
mi piace questo disegno, ma temo che il colore cambia.	m'areskee arketa to skhedion tooto, alla foboome mipos i bafi too ebgheni.
ho paura che questa stoffa non è di buon uso.	foboome mipos to ifasma tooto den eene stereon.
al contrarijo è eccellente.	ex enantias, eene excreton.
non potrà mai consumarla.	eparete to epi ti enghïisee moo.
potete prenderla sotte la mia parola.	den tha khalasee.
ora ditemi quante vi deve.	tera eepate mi pesa sas khreosto.
tutte ciò quanto costa ?	pesa kamnoon ola avta.
ecce è il vostro cento.	idoo o loghariasmos sas.
vengano a settanta due franchi.	to olon eene ebdominta dio franka.
non vi sbagliate ?	den ekhete lathes.
il cento è giuste, può centare voi stesso.	o loghariasmos eene orthos leghariasate ke mones.
ecco quatro Napolioni che fanno ottanta franchi, e datemi il resto.	idoo tessara Napolionis ta kamnoon oghdointa franka ekhete na mi dosite to eteros.
eccolo, Signore.	idoo avta, Kirie.
mandatemili subito.	steelate mi tavta amesos.
l'avrete in dieci minuti.	thelete ta ekhee entes deka lepton.

CON UN LIBRAJO.   META BIBLIOPOLON.

avete ricevuto ultimamente un assortimento dei libri Francesi desidero vederli.	elabete pro olighon keron silloghin Ghallikon biblion epethimoon na ta ido.

ENGLISH.	TURKISH.
Certainly, Sir.	bashim ùstuna effendim.
They were only unpacked this morning, you shall have the first view.	bù sàhaha dìghin ànlar chùzulma-mishdi àulari èvvèlā siz ghyùr-mish, òlajaksiniz.
Are they all new books?	jùmléssi yèni kìtābmidir.
Not all, Sir, some are new, others old publications.	khàyr effendim bà"zissi yèni vè bà"zissi èsski bàssmadir.
I hope you will find some to suit you.	in-shā-'llāh bà"zissi effendimin tāb"ina mùtābikdir.
Show the gentleman the books we have received recently.	ghèchenlarda ghèlan kìtābleri effendiya ghyùsster.
Well, Sir, do you find anything you like?	nàssl effendim zāt"ālīnza ghyùra kìtāb bùldunizmi.
Yes, here is a list of the books I wish to have.	èvvet bòldum ìshta bèni istedighim kìtāblerim pùsslassi bùdir.
Will you have them in boards or bound?	ànlari èjzāmi yòksa jìldlanmishmi isstersiniz.
I want them bound.	ànlari jildlanmish ìssterim.
What kind of binding do you wish?	né tùrlu jild isstersiniz.
Will you have them in calf or in cloth?	kàblari mèshinmi yòksa bùzaghi dèrissi òlsun.
I want this bound in morocco and gilt-edged.	bùnun kàbini sàkhtiyān vè kèmar-larini yàldizli isterim.
What colour will you have the morocco?	né rànkda sàkhtiyān istersiniz.
Is the price the same for all colours?	mèjmū" rànkin pàhassi bìrmidir.
The same, Sir, the colour makes no difference in price.	birdir effendim rènghdan pàhassi fàrk itmaz.
I will take care that they are done exactly as you direct.	tà"rīfiniz ùzéré dìkkātila jùm-léssini jildledirim effendim.
Do you want anything else?	dàha dìghir bìr shèy isstersiniz.
I should like a copy of Redhouse's Dictionary.	Redhouse nàm mù'èllifin lùghāt-kitābi issterim.
Have you Barker's Grammar?	sizda Barker lùghāt kitābi varmi.
I have one copy by me, which is in good condition, and not dear.	bìr mùsskha vàr dir vè hèm ghyùzèl vèhàmda ùjùzdir.
I prefer a new copy.	bèn yèngissini tèrjīh iderim.

ITALIAN.	GREEK.
molto volentieri Signore.	asmenos Kirie.
sono stati sballati questa mattina solamente, voi siete il primo di vederli.	simerou to proi ta ebghalamen apo ta kibotia, sees tha ta idete protes.
sono tutti libri nuovi ?	eene ola neofani biblia.
non Signore, alcuni sono nuovi ed altri di publicazione vecchia.	okhi Kirie, eene ke neofani ke palea.
spero che troverete di che essere contento.	elpiso na evrite tiavta ex on na evkharistithete.
fate vedere al Signore i libri che abbiamo ricevuto ultimamente.	deexate ees ton Kirien ta biblia, ta epia elabomen eskhatos.
ebbene Signore, trovate qualche cosa chè vi piacce ?	cerete lipen, Kirie, tipote tis ereskias sas.
si, ecco la lista dei libri che desidero avere.	malista, idoo simeeosis ton biblion osa epithimo na aghoraso.
vuolete che siano in cartone o legati ?	ta thelete adeta i demena.
si veglio legati.	ta thelo demene.
che specie di legatura desidera.	ti eedos desimatos epithimeete.
vuolete che siane in vitello o in foglio ?	ta thelete me moskharision tomarion i me probatoo.
desidero che questo sia legato in marroccho e i foglii dorati.	epithimo na dethi tooto memarokinon ke na khrisothi,ton filon.
di che colore vuele il marroccho ?	pioo khromatos thetete to marokinen.
il prezzo è lo stesse per tutti i colori ?	ola ta khromata ekoon tin avtin timin.
lo stesso Signore, il colore non fà nissuna differenza nel prezzo.	tin avtin Kirie, to khroma den metaballee kat'ooden tin timin.
bene Signore, saranno legati seconde il vostro desiderio.	malista Kirie,.tha frontiso na dethoon akribos apos epithimeete.
avete bisogna di qualche altra casa ?	khreeazesthe akemi tipotes.
veglio una copia del Dizionario di Redhouse.	ithela.en soma too lexikoo too Redhouse.
avete la Grammatica di Barker ?	ekhete to ghrammatikon too Barker.
ho una copia in buona condizione e non è cara.	ekho arketa kenoorion en soma ke okhi akribon.
preferisce una copia nuova.	to thelo kallion oles dioloo neon.

ENGLISH.	TURKISH.

It is impossible, the book is out of print.

múmkin dighildir effendim chùnku bassmeyurler.

It is now in the press.

bàsselmakdadir.

But nobody knows when it will appear.

làkin né wàket mèydāna ghelyur kìmsé bìlmaz.

If so, I had better secure your copy.

ùylé issé sizinkini àlmak dàha èvvela òlur.

What do you want for it?

àna né isstersiniz.

I wanted £2 10s. for it.

iki bùchuk àltin issterim.

But as you have purchased several other books, you shall have it for £2.

làkin siz dàha sā'ir kìtābler àlmish òldughinizdan iki àltina vèrerim.

Put it aside, and send it with the other books.

bìr tàrafa kàydan òlbir kìtāblerila bèrābèr ghyùnder.

Chapter XXIII.

APARTMENTS.

KIRA ODA DA'IRE.

Have you any apartments to let?

kirā òdalariniz vàrmidir.

Yes Sir, I have several; what rooms do you wish for?

èvvet effendim khàyli vàr hànghi òdalari isstersiniz.

Do you want apartments furnished or unfurnished?

dùshènmish òdalarimi yòkhsa dùshènmemishmi isstersiniz.

I want furnished rooms.

òdalari dùshènmish issterim.

I should like to have two bed rooms with a sitting room and kitchen.

bìr mùtfak bìr mùssāfir òdassi vè ikida yàtak òdasi issterim.

I can accommodate you, please walk in.

sizin istedighiniz bènda vàr kerem idub ichèri byùyùriniz.

I will show you the rooms. This is the sitting room.

sizè òdalari ghyùstereim ishta mùssāfir òdasi.

It is not very large, but it will do for me.

pèk òlkader byùyuk dèghildir amma bènim ichin èlverir.

You see there is everything necessary, and the furniture is very neat.

ghyùruyursiniz effendim her bìr shey mùkèmmèldir vè dùshèmada pèk zārifdir.

All the furniture is mahogany.

dùshèma hèp màghun àghajidir.

ITALIAN.	GREEK.

è impossibile perche il libro è fuori di stampa.

è ora nella stampa.

ma non si sà quando apparirá.

in questo caso meglio sicurare la vestra copia.

quante domandate?

vuoglio sessanta due franchi.

siccome avete comprato molti altri libri vi la darò per cinquanta franchi.

mettetelo a parte e mandatemilo cogli altri libri.

eene adinaton, dioti i ekdosis exintlithi.

eene tera ees ta piestiria.

all'eene adilon pete thelee dimosievthi.

en tiavti periptosse protimo na labo to antitipon to opien sees ekhete.

posa ziteete di' avto.

thelo exikonta dio franchi.

all'epeedi imees pernete ke alla biblia akemi, tha sas dino dia peninta franchi.

balete to kata meros, ke mi to stellete meta ton allon biblion.

APPARTAMENTI.

PERI KATIKIAS.

avete appartamento d'affitto?

si ginore, ne ho varii, che camere desiderate?

volete appartamento mobigliato, o senza mobiglie.

veglie camere mobigliate.

veglio due camere di dormire una sala ed una cucina.

posso accommodarvi, pregho entrate.

vi farò vedere le stanze ecco la sala.

non è grande ma mi basterà.

vedete Signore che v'é tutto quel che necessarie e le mobiglie sono nuovi.

tutte le mobiglie sono d'acajù.

ekhete domatia di enikiasma.

malista Kirie, epia domatia epithimeete.

thelete katikian me epipla i khoris epipla.

thelo demation me epipla.

thelo dio thomamatia too ipnoo me mian edoosan ke en magheereeon.

eemboro na sas ikonomiso labete ton kopon na eeselthite.

na sas deexo ta domatia idoo i edoosa.

den eene polla meghali alla eemboree na me khrisimevsi.

blebete oti ekhee òla ta anankea, ke oti ta epipla eene polli nea.

ola ta epipla eene apo maeni.

ENGLISH.	TURKISH.
Here are two armchairs, six chairs, a new carpet, a handsome glass, and pretty curtains.	ìshta iki kòltuklu sàndāliyyé Alti "ādī sàndāliyyé bìr yèngi hàli bìr à"là āyīné ghāyetla zārif pèrdéler.
Also there are cupboards on both sides of the fire-place.	vè bùnlardan mā"àdā òjaghin ìki tàraflarindada dòlab vàr dir.
Yes, there is all that I require.	èvvet effendim her bìr lèwāzimāt tèkmīldir.
Let me see the bed rooms?	yàtak òdalarini ghyùsteriniz.
This way, Sir, if you please.	bùradan kerem bùyyuriniz effendim.
Let us see if the bed is good, that is the main point.	bàkalim yàtak àyyimidir zīra òl bàshlija khùssùssdir.
When I have a good bed, I care little for the rest.	yàtaghim ràhat òldikdan sòngra bàshka shèyleri chòk bàkmam.
You cannot wish for a better.	bùndan à"lassini bòlamazsiniz.
Does the room face the street?	òdalar sòka-gha kàrshimidir.
No, Sir, it faces the garden.	khàyr effendim bàghchaya kàrshidir.
So much the better, I don't like to sleep in a front room, on account of the noise of carriages.	àyi dir "àraba shàmatassindan dòlayi sòkaghda kàrshi òdada ùyàmakdan hàzz itmam.
Do you wish to see the other room?	òlbìr òdayada ghyùrmèk isstermisiniz.
Now, the only question is about the price.	shindi yàliniz bir bazarlik sù'āli kàldi.
What do you ask for the three rooms and the kitchen?	ùch òda vè mùtfak ichin nè isstersiniz.
I have always let the parlour with one of the rooms for fourteen shillings.	mùssāfir òdassila yàtak òdalarindan birini dā'imā òn dùrt shillina vèriyurum.
Will you give me a guinea a week for the whole?	màjmū"i ichin sizdan hàftalighina bìr lira vè bir shilli issterim.
It is only seven shillings for the other room and the kitchen.	mùtfakila òl bìr òda siza yèdi shillina ghèlir.
I think it a great deal of money.	chòk pàhalli zàn iderim.

ITALIAN.

ecce due sedie a bracciuoli, sei sedie un tappeto nuove, un bello specchio e cortini molto polite.

anche vi sono armai alle due latte del camminetto.
si v'è tutto che è necessarie.

fatemi vedere le camere di dormire.
favorisca di venire di questa parte.

vediamo se il lette è polito questa è la principale cosa.
quando ho un buon lette, non mi curo del resto.
non potete desiderare meglio.

la camera si facia strada?

non Signore, si facia al giardino.

molte meglio, non mi piace dormire rimpetto la strada per causa del rumore delle carrozze.

volete vedere l'altra stanza?

non si tratta adesso altro che del prezzo.
quanto volete per le tre camere colla cucina?
ho sempre affittato il salene con una delle camere quatordici franchi.
volete paghare venti un scellini la settimana per tutti?
sono solamente sette scellini per l'altra camera e la cucina.

mi pare è molto caro.

GREEK.

idoo dio polithrones ex kathikle, ees evmorfos kathreptis ke parapetasmata evprepi.

pros tootis eene ke armaria ees ta plagkia tis estias.
malista eene ola ta anankea.

deexate mi toos kitonas.

ap' edo, Kirie, orisate.

na ido an ine i klini kali, dioti tooto eene to protiston.
etan ekho kalin klinin den me melee dia t' alla.
den eemboreete na epithimisete kalliteran.
blebee to domation ees ton dromon.
òkhi, Kirie, blebee pros ton kipon.

toson kalliteron, den aghapo na kimome ees to prosopon ton ikion eneka too thoriboo ton amaxon.
thelete na idite to allo domation.

tora menee monen peri tis timis na simfonisomen.
ti ziteete dia ta tria domatia me to magheerion.
pantote tin edoosan me en ton demation enikiaza dia dekatessara franka.
tha plirosete d'ela mian ghi-inean tin ebdomada.
den eene para epta silinia dia to allo domation ke to magheereeon.
nomizo oti eene poli.

ENGLISH.	TURKISH.

Consider that this is one of the best quarters of the town, where the houses are let at very high rents.

tèfèkkyur bùyùriniz effendim bùr-assi shèhrin èn ì"tibārli yèri òldùghùndan èvlerin kìrāssi zìyādédir.

Well, I will give you one pound.

hèr né issa siza bìr lira vèrerim.,

But I must have a part of the cellar, and a place to put coals and wood in.

làkin màkhzendan bìr-àz yèr ìla kyùmur vè òdun kòyajak yer issterim.

That is understood, you shall have a place with a lock and key to it.

òrassi mà"lūm ànakhtàr vé kìli-dila siza bir màhàll vèririm.

When do you mean to take possession of your lodging?

bù sūrètta effendim bù òdalara né wàkit ghèlup òturajaksiniz.

I intend to come and sleep here to-night.

bù àksham bùraya ghèlup yàtmak nìyyèt ideyurim.

See that everything is ready.

bakki hèr shèy hàzir òlsun.

Very well, Sir, you can come as soen as you please.

bàsh ùstuné effendim isstedighiniz wàkit tèshrīf bùyuriniz.

CHAPTER XXIV.

WITH AN UPHOLSTERER.	DUSHEMEJI ILA.

I wish to look at some furniture.

bà"zi dùshéméler ghyùrmek isste-rim.

Please walk in, Sir, I think I can suit you.

ìchèri bùyurun effendim, zàn iderim sizlera ghyùra vàr dir.

What sort of furniture do you wish to see?

né tùrlu dùshémé isstersiniz.

I want a book-case, if I can find a neat one.

hàrīfindan bùlur issam bìr kìtāb-hané issterim.

Here is a very fine one.

ishta siza ghyùzèl bir kìtābhané effendim.

I bought it yesterday at a sale.

àni dùn mèzāddan àldim.

It is made of beautiful wood.

àghaji pèk ghyùzèl dir.

How much do you ask for it?

àna né isstersiniz.

The price is twelve guineas.

pàhassi òn ìki lìra vè òn ìki shillin dir.

ITALIAN.	GREEK.
considerando Signore, che questo è il miglior quartiere della città e le rendite sono cari.	silloghisthite oti edo eene en ton kallisten meron tis poleos ke e ikie timonte ipermetros.
ebbene vi darò una lira.	kala sas dido mian ghi-inean.
ma però veglio una parte della cantina ed un luogo per mettere legno e carbone.	alla me khreeazete en meros too ipogheeoo ke en meros dia na ballo xila ke karboona.
è ben inteso Signore avrà un luogo con chiave.	tooto ennoeete. tha ekeete en meros to opien na kleedonete.
quando verrà a occupare il vostro appartamento ?	pete meletate na elthete ees tin katikian sas.
intendo venire a dormire questa nette.	skopevo na eltho na kimitho apopse edo.
fatte tutto pronto.	frontisate na ine ta panta etima enoris.
si Signore, potrà venire quando le piace.	arkee, Kirie, dinasthe na elthite ama thelisete.

COL VENDITORE DI MOBIGLIE.	META EPIPLOPION.
desidero a vedere alcuni mobiglie.	ithela na ido merika epipla.
favorisca entrate Signore, crede che vi posso accomodare.	kopiasate mesa, Kirie, nomizo oti eemboro na sas evkharistiso.
che specie di mobiglie desidera a vedere.	ti epipla epithimeete na idite.
veglie una biblioteca se troverò una in buona condizione.	thelo mian bibliothikin, an tin evre evprepee.
ecce una è molte bella.	idoo mia polla orea.
l'ho comprata jeri al' incanto.	tin aghorasa khthes ees mian dimo-prasian.
è d'un legno molte bello.	eene apo xilon exereton.
che prezzo volete ?	pesa ziteete di' avti.
il prezzo è dodici guinea.	i timi tis eene dodeka ghi-ine-c.

Now I should like to look at a chest of drawers.

shindi bìr chèkméjé ghyùrmek issterim.

A double or a single one?

yàln-kàtmi yòksa ìki kàtmi olsun.

Here are several, with the prices marked upon each.

ìshta siza ànwà"i pàhalarida ùyerinda dir ìshārèt òlinmish dir.

I think I shall fix upon this.

ghāliba bìmi bèghenejaghim.

Now let me see your carpets.

shindi kìlimlerinizi ghyùraim.

What size do you want?

né bòyda òlsun.

Six yards by five.

àlti àrshin bòy òlsun vè bèsh àrshin āni olsun.

Here are some of all sorts.

ishta ànlardan hèr bìr tùrlussi.

These are very costly.

bùnlar pàhallidir.

Here are some cheaper; but they are, of course, neither so handsome nor so good.

ishta ùjūzleri lakin ànlara òlbirleri kadar ghyùzél dir vé néda òl kàdar àyi dir.

I should like this well enough, but it is so expensive.

bùndan òldukja hàz ittim àmmā khàylija àkchaya tèwàkkuf ider.

No, Sir, you will think it very cheap, if you consider how large it is.

khàyr effendim ègher bòyini dùshunsaniz chòk ùjūz dir derriniz.

Should you like to look at some second-hand?

bà"zi kùllanilmishlarini ghyùrmek isstermisiniz.

No, I will take this.

khàyr bùni àlirim.

Do you want anything else?

bàshka bìr shèy isstermisiniz.

What price are these chairs?

bù sàndālìyyélerin pàhassi kàchdir.

They are two guineas each.

ànlar ìki līra.

They ought to be good at that price.

òl pàhaya ghyùra ànlar àyi òlmalidir.

These are very beautiful chairs.

bùnlar pèk zàrīf sàndālìyyélerdir.

These chairs are of the first quality, and in the newest fashion.

bù sàndāllìyyéler bìrinji sày ve èn yèngi tàrzda dir.

Consider that they are made of the finest wood and highly finished.

mùlāhaza bùyurun àghaji ghāyetla ·ghyùzèl vè ishi pèk à"la và ayi dir.

They were made by the best workmen in London.

ànlar lòndrada bìrinji ùsstanin ìshidir.

I like the chairs very well, but not the price.

sàndāllìyyélardan pèk hàz ittim làkin pàhassini bèghenmeyurim.

I shall put off this purchase till another time.

bù àlish vèrish bàshka vàkta bràkayim.

ITALIAN.	GREEK.
ora vorrei vedere un commodo.	tera ithela na ido ena kemon.
doppio o uno semplice?	diploon i menen.
ecco sono molti col prezzo marchate sopra ciascuno.	idoo diafora me tin timin simocomenin epano ton.
forse mi fisserò sopra questo.	nomizo oti tooto tha protimiso.
mostratemi ora i tapetti.	tora na ido tees tapitas sas.
di che grandezza li volete?	pioo meghethoos aghapate.
sei jarde di lunghezza e 5 di larghezza.	ex metron mikoos ke pente platoos.
ecce d'egni sorte.	idoo pantoos eedoos.
questi sono molto cari.	avton i timi anabenee ipsila.
ecce alcuni che sono più buon mercato, ma non sono cosi belli neppure cosi buoni.	idoo ke evthinoteri, alla fisiko to logho den eene oote toson evmorfi oote toson kali.
mi piace questo ma è molto caro.	m'areskee arketa avtos edo, all'eene peli akripos.
non Signore, mi pare è buon mercato si guardate la grandezza.	okhi Kirie, tha ton evrete evthinon, analoghos pros to meghethos too.
volete vedere ad alcuni di seconde mane?	thelete na idate tis evkerias (i metakheerismenoos).
no, prenderò questo.	okhi, perno teeton.
volete qualche altra cosa?	khreeazesthe alle ti.
quanto è il prezzo di queste sedie?	ti timis eene avte e kathikle.
due lire l'une.	dio ghi-ineas timate pasa mia.
devono essere buoni a questo prezzo.	dinaton na ine kale di' avtin tin timin.
queste sedie sono bellissime.	avte e kathikle eene exereti.
queste sedie sono di prima qualità e alla moda.	avte e kathikle eene tis protis piotitos ke kata ton televteon sirmon.
vedete che sono del più bel legno, e sono perfetti.	blebete oti eene apo to kalliston xilon ke i erghasia ton entelestati.
sono fatti dal migliore lavoratore in Londra.	kateskevasthisan apen ton iriston tekhnitin too Londinoo
mi piaceno le sedie ma sono molto cari.	m' areskoon arketa e kathikle, all' okhi ke i timi ton.
farò questa comprata un' altra volta.	tha anabalo tin aghoran tavtin ees allote.

ENGLISH.	TURKISH.
Well, you will send these things as soon as possible.	ìmdi, siz bùnlari èvima imkyāni mèrtébé chàbik ghyùnder.
You shall have them in the course of the day.	bù ghyùn ùhinda ànlar tàrafiniza wāssil òlur.
Do not disappoint me.	sàkin bèni àldatmayassin.
You may depend upon it.	ì"timād òlsun.

CHAPTER XXV.

TO BUY SEVERAL ARTICLES.	ESHYA SATIN-ALMAK.
Will you come to town with me?	bènim ila chàrshi ghidermisiniz.
With all my heart.	bàshim ùsstuna effendim.
What have you to do in town?	chàrshida né ìshiniz vàr dir.
I want to go to the linen-draper's.	bèzjí dùkkyànnà (dùkéna) ghìtmek issterim.
I have a few things to buy.	bìr kàch shèy àlajaghim vàr.
What do you want to buy?	né àlajaksiniz.
I want some lace.	bìr-àz shèrīd àlmak issterim.
I want some calico.	bìr-àz bèza mùhtājim.
I must get some sheeting.	bìr-àz chàrshaflik bèz àlmaliim.
Do you not want to buy anything yourself?	siz kendiniz ichin bà"zi shèy àlmayajakmisiniz.
Not anything in particular.	màkhsūss bìr shèy àlajak dighilim.
Perhaps we may see some new prints.	bèlki bà"zi yèngi bàssmaler ghyùruriz.
Don't let me forget to buy some handkerchiefs.	bèni ùnùtirmayasiniz bìr-àz yèmènī vè chèvrè àlmak issterim.
I will remind you of it.	àni khātiriniza ghètiririm.
Let us go directly, for we must be back for tea.	hàman shìndi ghìdalim zìra chày ìtchmek wàktina "àvdet etmaliiz.
We have fully an hour before us.	tàmām bìr sà"at wàktiniz vàr dir.
We shall be back before that time.	òl wàkta kàdar "àvdet ideriz.

ITALIAN.	GREEK.
ebbene mi manderete quelle cese il più presto possibile.	kala, na mi tas seelete osen takhista.
l'avrete nella giornata.	tha sas ekhete entes tis imeras.
non ingannatemi.	mi me apatisete.
statevi sicuro.	min ekhete ennian.

PER COMPRARE VARII OGGETTI.	AGHORAS DIAFORON PROGHMATON.
volete venire con me alla città ?	thelete na elthete ees tin polin mazi moo.
volentieri.	malista, meta khara.
che cosa avete a fare nella città ?	ti tha kamete ees tin polin.
deve andare al magazine di novità.	ekho na ipagho ees ton emboron ton meoteron eeden.
veglie comprare alcune cese.	ekho na kame tinas aghoras.
che cosa volete comprare ?	ti tha aghorasete.
veglie comprare alcuni merletti.	thelo n'aghoraso dantellas.
ho bisogna di calico.	khreeazome amerikanikon pani.
veglie tela per lenzuole.	prepee n' aghoraso pani dia sindonia.
non volete comprare niente per voi stesso ?	den ekhete ke sees n' aghorasite tipote.
nulla di particulare.	eeden axion loghoo.
forse vedremo nuovi disegni d' indiana.	isos idomen nea deeghmata indianon.
non fatemi scordare di comprare alcuni fazzoletti.	na m' enthimisete n' aghoraso mandilia.
vi ramenterò.	tha sas enthimiso.
andiamo subito, bisogna ritornare nel tempo per il te.	as kinisomen ameses, dioti prepee na eemetha palin edo ees to te-i.
abbiamo ancora un ora.	ekhomen da keron mias oras.
ritorneremo in tempo.	tha eemetha edo pro tis oras tavtis.

Chapter XXVI.

WITH A TAILOR.	TERZI ILA.
I have sent for you to measure me for a coat.	bìr sètri ichin ùlchumi àlasiniz dèyé sìzi chàghirtim.
Will you take my measure for a coat?	bìr sètri ìchin ùlchumi àlirmisiniz.
How will you have it made?	nàssl yàpilssin.
Make it as they wear them now.	shìndiki "àdeta ghyùra yàpiniz.
You want also the waistcoat and trousers.	pàntalon vè yèlekda isstersiniz.
Yes, I bought the cloth to have a complete suit.	èvvet tãmm bìr kàt rùba ìchin chòha àldim.
Very well, sir, how do you wish to have your waistcoat made?	pèk àyi effendim, yèlek né bìchimda òlsun.
Make it after the present fashion.	shìndiki mòda nàsslissa ùylé òlsun.
What sort of buttons will you have?	né tùrlu dùymé isstersiniz.
I will have them covered with the same stuff.	kèndi chòhasindan issterim.
Very well.	pàsh ùsstuna effendim.
Make me a pair of trousers with straps.	pàntalon sùpiyali òlsun.
Make them wide, I like to be at my ease.	pàntaloni ghènishja yàpiniz bèn ràhatimi sèverim.
Never fear.	hìch dùshùmayasiniz.
Would you like your trousers to come very high?	pàtalon chòk yùkāri ghelsinmi.
Not too high, nor too low.	né pèk yùkāri vé nèda pèk àshaghi òlsun.
They shall be made exactly as you like.	sìzin ìsstedighiniz ghibi yàparim.
Remember that I must have this by next Tuesday without fail.	bòsha chìkmamak ùzéré búni pàzār ghyùni ichin issterim khàtirinizda òlsun.
You shall have it on Tuesday morning.	sàli ghyùnun sàbāhi ghètiririm.

ITALIAN.

GREEK.

CON UN SARTORE.

ho mandato a chiamarvi per prendere la mia mesura per farmi un abito.

prendete la mia misura per un vestito.

come volete che sia fatta ?

fatemelo come si usano oggi.

volete anche i calzoni ed il gilè.

si, ho comprato panno per un vestimento intiere.

sarà servita Signore, come volete che il gile sarà fatta ?

fatilo alla moda.

che specie di bottoni volete ?

si veglie della medesima stoffa.

molto bene.

fatemi un paio di pantaloni con staffe.

fateli larghi, perche voglie essere al mio comede.

non tema, Signore.

volete che i vostri pantaloni montano assai ?

ne troppo alto ne troppo basso.

saranno fatti secondo del suo gusto.

ricordatevi che veglio questi martedi senza dubbio.

l'avrà martedi mattina senza dubbio.

META RAPTOO.

esteela ke sas ekraxa dia na moo parete metron di' en forema.

parakalo na moo parete metron di' en forema.

pos to thelete.

kamete moo to opos sinithizonte.

thelete omoo ghelekon ke pantalenion.

malista, ighorasa rookhon di' olokliron endimasian.

arkee tooto, Kirie, pos thelete to ghelekon.

kamete to too meoo sirmoo.

ti kombia thelete.

thelo kombia apo to avto ifasma.

poli kala.

kamete moo en pantaloni me ipodesmoos.

kamete to arketa plati, den thelo na me stenokhori.

mi fobisthe.

thelete to pantaloni na anabeni poli ipsila.

oote ipsila oote khamila.

tha sas ta kamo kata tin areskeean sas.

na enthimisthe oti ta thelo tin tetartin afevktos.

tha ta ekhete tin titartin pro-i.

ENGLISH.	TURKISH.
Mind, if you disappoint me, this will be the last work you do for me.	bàk dùshunin ègher bèni àlda-dirsiniz bìr dàha àsslan sàna ìsh vèrmam.
Have you brought my coat?	sètrimi ghètirdimni.
Yes, Sir, here it is.	èvvet effendim ìshta.
You are a man of your word, but I began to grow impatient.	sèn sùzinda kàvī bìr àdemsin bènim-issa sàbrim dùkènmagha bàshlamish idi.
It is but ten o'clock, and I had promised it you some time in the morning.	sà"āt fàkat òudir bèn àni siza bù sàbāh ìchin và"īd ìtmishidim.
Let me try it on.	ghètir àni tèjribé idaim.
Let us see how it fits.	bàkalim nàssl ghèlir.
You have made the sleeves too long and too wide.	kòllarini hèm ùzūn vè hèmda bòl.
Sir, they wear them very large now.	effendim, kòllarin chòk bòl òlmassi shindi "àdet dir.
It is too narrow.	dàr dir.
It pinches me under the arms.	kòltuk àltarimi sìkiyur.
It cuts my arms.	kòllarimi kèssiyur.
Is it not rather long?	bìr-āz ùzūnja dighílmi dir.
It seems to me a little too long.	bàna bìr-āz ùzūnja ghyùriniyur.
It is too long-waisted.	bèli ùzūndir.
It is too short-waisted.	bèli kissadir.
It is in wrinkles between the shoulders.	òmuzlari àrassinda bùt dùriyur.
You cannot complain of this coat.	bù sètridan shèkwà idamazsiniz.
It fits you extremely well.	siza pèk àyi ghèldi.
You tailors never find fault with your own work.	siz tèrziler ishinizda àssla kùssūr bòlamazsiniz.

CHAPTER XXVII.

WITH A SHOEMAKER.	KUNDURAJI ILA.
I want a pair of shoes.	bìr chìft kùndura ìssterim.
Will you measure me for a pair of shoes?	bìr chift kundura ichin ùlchumi àl.
I have your measure already.	sizin ùlchunizi bènda vàr dir.

ITALIAN.	GREEK.

badate di non mancare altrimenti sarebbe l'ultimo lavoro che farete per me.

prosexate dioti an athetisite ton loghon sas, tha eene avti i televtea moo paranghelia ees esas.

avete portate il mio abito?

eferete to forema moo.

si Signore, eccolo.

malista Kirie idoo avto.

siete uomo di parola, ma vi dirò chiaramente ho quasi perse la mia pazienza.

efilaxete ton loghon sas. Sas legho omes elevtheros oti eekh' arkhisee na eeme anipomonos.

sono solamente le dieci vi ho promesso di portarle la mattina. .

eene tora olighoteron ton deka, ke egho sas to eekha iposkhethe kata tas pro mesimbrias oras.

datemilo di provarlo.

na to dokimaso.

vediamo come và.

as idomen pos m' ipaghi.

avete fatto le maniche molto lunghe e molto larghe.

ekamete ta manikia para makria ke para platia.

Signore, oggi è la moda d'avergli grandi.

tora, Kirie, poli meghala sineethizonte.

è troppo stretto.

me eene para stenon.

mi stringe sette le braceie.

me stenevee ipo tas maskhalas.

mi serra le braceie.

moo koptee toos brakhionas.

non è un poco lunghe?

den eene olighon makri.

mi pare che è un poco lunghe.

mi fenete olighon para makri.

è molto lungho nel taglio.

eene makri ees tin mesin.

è molto curto nel taglio.

ekhee para kontin tin mesin.

si piegha fra le spalle.

kamnee soofres anamesa ees toos amees.

Signore, non può biasmare di questo abito.

den dinasthe na paraponethite dia tooto to forema.

le va molto hene.

sas pighenee excreta.

voi sartori non trovate mai nissun sbaglio ne' vostri laveri.

sees i rapte pote den evriskete fsalma ees ta ergha sas.

CON UN CALZOLAJO.

META IPODIMATOPIOO.

veglie un paio di scarpe.

khreeazome en zevgho ipodimata.

volete misurarmi per un paio di scarpe?

iarete moo, parakalo, metron di' en zevghari embadon.

ne ho di già la vostra misura.

ekho idi to metron sas.

ENGLISH.	TURKISH.
Take good care to make them wide enough.	hiyadé dikat it bòlja òlssun.
Do not make them too narrow.	dàr òlmassun.
Never fear, Sir.	hìch kòrkmaniz effendim.
That is your fault, you generally make them too narrow.	sizlerin "àdetiniz dir èksèriyyā pèk dàr yàpiyùrsiniz.
I will take care to make these according to your wish.	bù dèf"à èmriniz ùzère yàpmagha dikat iderím.
When can you let me have them?	ànlari né wàkit bàna tèsslīm ìdersiniz.
I will send them towards the end of the week.	hàftanin nìhāyetina dùghri ànlari siza irsāl idarim.
You shall have them by the beginning of next week.	ghèlejak hàftanin ìbtidāsinda siza ànlari tèslīm idarim.
Do not disappoint me.	bèni àldatma.
You may rely upon my premise.	wà"dima ì"timād idiniz effendim.
Are you in want of anything else?	bàshka bìr shèy isstermisiniz.
Now I think of it, I want a pair of dress boots.	shìndi "àklima gèldi mùssāfirligha ghìtmek ùhin bìr chìft chìzma ìssterim.
I should also like to have a pair of slippers.	bìr chìftta pàbuch issterim.
Of what do you wish them made?	né dan òlsun.
I want them in morocco leather.	à"la sàkhtiyāndan òlsun.
Make them as quickly as possible.	ìmkyāni mèrtébé ànlari chàbik bìtir.
Sir, I have brought your shoes.	effendim sizin kùnduralarinizi ghètirdim.
Let me see them.	ghyùraim.
Allow me to try them on you.	rùkhsatiniz ìla ànlari àyakiniza ghìderaym.
No thank you, I will try them on myself.	khàyr tèshèkkyur iderim bèn kèndim ànlari tèjribé iderim.
I cannot get my feot in.	àyaghim ghìrmayur.
Here is a shoe horn.	ishta bìr kùndura chèkajek vàr.
I must have shoes that I can put on without any trouble.	bènim ghiyajaghim kùnduralari bèn zàhmetsizja ghìmek issterim.

ITALIAN.	GREEK.
badate di farli abbastanza larghe.	prosexate na ghinoon platea.
non fatteli molto streete.	mi ta kamete stena.
non ha paura, Signore.	mi sas meli, Kirie.
questo è il vostro diffetto che generalmente molto stretti.	ekhete sees tooto to elattora, zinithos ta kamnete stena stenotera too deontos.
prenderò molto cura di farli come lei desidera.	tha frontiso na ghinoon tis ghnomis sas.
quando potrete farmi avergli?	pete tha imboresete na mi ta dosite.
vi le manderò verso la fine della settimana.	tha sas ta steelo pres to teles tis ebdomados.
le avrete nel principio della settimana veniente.	tha ta ekhete ees tas arkhas tis prosekhoos ebdomados.
non mancatemi.	mi leepsete omes.
potete dipendere sulla mia promessa.	sas to iposkhome exapantos.
avete bisogna di qualche altra cosa?	ekhete khrian alloo tinos.
adesso mentre mi ricordo veglio un paio di stivali settili.	tora enthimoome oti moo khriasete en zevkharion kalon ipodimaton.
vorrei anche avere un paio di pantofli.	ithela ke 'en zevkhari sirtes pantofles.
di che materie le volete che siano fatti?	apo ti tas thelete.
le veglio di marrocano.	tas ithela apo marokinon.
fatele il più presto possibile.	kamete tas oson takhista.
Signore, ho portato le vostre scarpe.	Kirie, sas fero tas embadas sas.
fatemi vederle.	na sas ido.
permettetemi di provarvile.	stathite na sas tas dokimaso.
no grazie, veglio provarle io.	okhi sas evkharisto, thelo mones moo na tas dokimaso.
il mio piede non può entrare.	ton poda moo den embasin.
eccolo una calzatoia.	idoo ees ipodima tosirtis.
devo avere di scarpe che posso metterli a piede.con commodità.	me khreeazonte embades, tas opias na eemboro na ballo elevtheros.

|

Why have you made them so pointed ? It is not the fashion.

I beg your pardon, they are worn so at present.

Very well, but I cannot put myself to any inconvenience for the sake of the fashion.

Decidedly, they are too tight.

They are a great deal too narrow.

They hurt my toes.

You have made them too pointed.

They hurt me.

They will grow wide enough by wearing.

This leather stretches like a glove.

Yes, but I do not wish to be crippled until they grew wider.

I cannot walk in them.

You will not have worn them two days before they cease to hurt you.

I have told you many times that I do not like to be pinched in my shoes.

I do not wish to get corns.

The leather is bad.

The upper leather is good for nothing.

The soles are too thin.

The quarters are too low.

The heels are a good deal too wide.

I am sure these shoes were never made for me.

Take them back, and make me another pair as soon as possible.

Have you brought my boots ?

---

nichiu bù kàdar sùri yàptinizòl shindi "àdet dìghildir.

"àfv idiniz effendim shindi ùylé ghiyiyurler.

bù sūrètda "ādetin khātiri ichin kìndimi bèn sìkindiya kàymam.

hàkīkat bùnlar pèk dàr dir.

ziyadasila ānsizdir.

àyaghimin pàrmaklarini àjidiyur.

pèk sèvri yàptiniz.

àyakimi injidiyur.

ghìya ghìya àchilirler.

bù sàkhtiyān èldivèn ghibi àchilir.

èvvet, àmmā ànlar àchilinjaya kadar isstamam ghyùturum òlaym.

bù kùndura ila yùruyameyurim.

ànlari iki ghyùn ghìymazdan èvvel àjitmelari kèssilir.

siza tèkrār bé-tèkrār dedimki kùnduranin pàrmaklarini sìkmassindan hàz itmam.

àyaklarimda nàssir bòghlamassini isstamam.

sàkhtiyāni fènadir.

yùz sàkhtiyāni hich bìr shèy dighil dir.

tàbanlari ghāyetla ìnja dir.

yàulari pèk àshàghi dir.

ùkchéleri pèk ànnli dir.

àyi bìlirim bù kùnduraler bènim ichin yàpilmamish dir.

bùnlari ghèri ghètir vè chàbikja bàna bàshka bir chìft yàp.

chìzmalerimi ghètirdinmi.

ITALIAN.	GREEK.
perchè l'avete fatto cosi puntati? mi pare che non è la moda.	diati tas ekamete toson soobleras, den eene too sirmoo.
dimande perdono, Signore, si fanno cosi adesso.	me sinkhoreete, kate to paren tiavtas foroon.
va bene, ma però non veglio incommodarmi per l'amore della moda.	esto, alla den thelo egho kharin too sirmoo na stenokhorome.
certamente sono molte stretti.	eene bebeon oti me spinghoon poli.
mi sono molto stretti.	eene para stene.
mi fanno male alle dita dei piedi.	moo plighonoon ta daktila.
l'avete fatto molto puntati.	tas ekamete pela soobleras.
mi fanno male.	me enokhloon.
s'allargheranno anche molto depo d'averli portati peche vuelte.	tha aplosoon osen tas foreete.
questa pelle si apre come la pelle del quante.	to derma tooto endidee osan ta kheeroktia.
si, ma finche s'allarghino non veglio mica essere storpiato (devenire zeppo).	ne, all' eos os aplosoon den thelo na khelene.
non posso caminare con queste scarpe.	den tha eemboro na peripatiso me avta.
depo d'averli portati due giorni non vi faranno più del male.	molis ta foresete dio imeras ke pleon den tha sas plighonoon.
vi ho detto molte volte che non veglio le scarpe siano stretti.	sas eepa idi pollakis, oti den thelo na eeme stenokhorimenos ees tas embadas moo.
non voglie avere dei calli.	den thelo na khamo kaloos.
la pelle è cattiva.	to tomari eene kakon.
la parte di sopra non vale niente.	to epano derma den axizee tipote.
le semelle sono molto sottili.	ta pelmata eene polla lepta.
i lati sono molto passi.	to opiso meros eene poli khamila.
i taleni di queste scarpe sono molto larghe.	ta takoonia eene para platea.
sone certo che queste scarpe non sono fatte per me.	eeme bebeos oti e embades avti den kateskevasthisan di' eme.
portateli via e fateme un altro paio il più presto possibile.	parete tas opiso, ke kamete mi en allo zevkhari osen takhista.
avete portate le mie stivali?	eferete ta ipodimata moo.

ENGLISH.	TURKISH.
Yes, Sir, here they are.	èvvet effendim ìshta.
The leg of this boot is too high.	bù chizmanin kònji ùzūndir.
I told you to make the heels very high.	ùkcheleri pèk yùksek òlsun dèyé siza sùwèyledim.
I cannot bear low heels.	àlchàk ùkchedan àssla hàz itmam.
Take these boots, they want new fronting.	bù chèzmayi ghètur ànlar yèni yùz isster.
That pair wants soling and heeling.	ò chìft hem yèni tàban vè hèmda yèni ùkché isster.
Half-sole these shoes.	bù kùnduraya yàrim tàban kòyin.
Do not forget to put a few nails in them.	ùnùtma ànlarin ichin bìr kàch ènkser kòy.
Send them back soon.	ànlari chàbik ghèri ghyùnder.

CHAPTER XXVIII.

WITH A PHYSICIAN.	BIR HEYKIM ILA.
I have taken the liberty to send for you.	effendim rùkhsatiniza màghruran siza khàber ghyunderub chàghìrtim.
I am afraid I need your assistance.	kòrkarim sizin ì"ānéniza mùhtājim.
How are you now?	shindi nàsslsiniz.
I do not know, I do not feel well.	bènda bìlmiyurim kindimi nàssl bùldighimi bènda bìlmiyurim.
My head is giddy, and I can hardly stand.	bàshim dùniyur vè àyak ùzerinda dùrmagha kùdretim yòk ghibidir.
I am not at all well.	hich àyi dèghilim.
I feel very ill.	kèndimi pèk khàssta hiss idiyurim.
I am extremely weak.	dèréjéssiz zà"fètim vàr.
How long have you been ill?	né wàketanbèri nā-mìzājssiz.
How were you taken ill?	mizājssizlighiniz nàssl bàshladi.
It began the day before yesterday by shivering fits.	dùn dìghil òlbìr ghyùn bìr tìtrémekla bàshladi.
Then I perspired profusely, and have been ill ever since.	sougra sèl ghìbi bìr tèr dìr bòshandi ìshta àndanberi khasstaim.

ITALIAN.	GREEK.

si Signore, eccoli.

la gamba di questo stivale è molte alta.

vi ho detto di fare i taleni molto alti.

non mi piacino i taleni bassi.

prendete queste stivalli e rimonta-teli.

questo paio bisogna che sia riso-rato.

mettete mezzo suole a queste scarpe.

non scordate di mettere pochi piccoli chiodi.

ritornatemeli presto.

malista Kirie, idoo avta.

to ano meros tootoo too ipodimatos eene poli ipsilon.

sas ipa na kamite ta takoonia poli ipsila.

den eemboro na ipofero ta khamila takoonia.

parete avta ta ipodimata ke akh-narite avtis.

tooto to zevkhari khreeazeste alla akhnaria.

balete misa akhnoria ees tavtas tas embadas.

mi lismonisete na balete merika karfia.

ke na mi ta ferete eghrighora.

CON UN DOTTORE.

META YATROO.

Signore, ho preso la libertà di mandare a chiamarvi.

elaba, Kirie, to tharros ke ezeela na sas kraxe.

ho bisogno del vostro aiuto.

ekho ananghin tis bo-itheeas sas.

adesso come state.

non sò, non mi sento bene.

pos evriskesthe tavtin tin stighmin.

den ixevro, eeme den ixevro pos.

la mia testa è sbalordita, e non posso stare a piedi.

ekho zalismenin tin kefalin ke diskolevome na stathe cestees podas.

non mi sento affatto bene.

mi sento molto male.

den ceme dioloo kala.

disthanome ton eavton moo lian astheni.

sono debolissimo.

da guando tempo siete malato?

come è cominciata la vostra malatia.

cominciò avanti jeri con trimore.

ekho meghistin adinamian.

apo pete eesthi arrestes.

pos ipon i arkhi.

prokhthes me en righos.

poi ho traspirato molte e di là fina ad orà sono malato.

epeeta idrosa poli, ke apo tote ceme olon kaka.

8

Did you feel a nausea?
yùrek bùlanmassi hiss ìttinizmi.

Yes, at first, but that went off, and I have had a terrible headache ever since.
èvvet ìbtidādé hiss ìttim lākin ò ghèchdi vé àndanberi pèk fèna bìr bàsh àghrissi ghèldi.

Where do you feel pain now?
shìndi nèreda zàhmet hiss idiyurssiniz.

I have pains in my head.
bàshimda àghri vàr.

My head aches terribly, I feel sick.
bàshim ziyadassila àghirir, ghyùngulim bùlaniyur.

I have a pain in my stomach.
kàrnim bìr vèjà hiss idiyurim.

I have a sore throat.
bòghāzim àghriyur.

I have been shivering all night.
bùtun ghèyjé titrèdim.

I feel pain in my side, and I breathe with difficulty.
yàn tàratimda àghri vàr vè ghyùjila nèfess àliyurim.

How is your appetite?
ìshtihāniz nàssl dir.

I have hardly eaten anything these two days.
ìki ghyùn dìr hàmān hich bìr shèy yèmadim.

Let me see your tongue.
dìlini ghyùraim.

Your tongue is foul.
dìliniz bùzukdir.

The stomach is loaded.
mì"dèniz dòlghyundir.

You must take a little medicine.
bìr-àz "ìlāj yèmalissiniz.

Let me feel your pulse.
nàbazana-bàkayim.

Your pulse is a little flurried.
nàbaziniz bìr-àz chàbìk dir.

Your pulse is hard, there is fever.
nàbaziniz sèrt dir bìr-àz hàrārèt vàr dir.

You are feverish.
hàrārètiniz vàr dir.

Do you think my illness dangerous?
khàsstalighim kòrkulimi zàn idermissiniz.

No, but you must take care lest it should become so.
khàyr lākin kindinizi sàkiniz òl dèréjéya ghèlmasin.

What am I to do?
nè ideyim.

I will send you something to take, and see you again to-morrow morning.
siza ìchejak bìr shèy ghyùnderirim vè yàrin sàbāhda ghèlib sizi tèkrer ghyùrurim.

Must I do anything further?
bàshka bìr shèy yàpajaghimmi.

No, only take care to keep yourself warm.
khàyr fàkat kèndinizi sìjàk hìfz idiniz.

ITALIAN.	GREEK.

avete avuto nausea?

isthanthite navtiasin.

si, al cominciamento ma dopo peco è passate e mi ha lasciato con gran dolore di testa.

ne, tin protin sighmin all' isteron parilthe tooto ke mi emeene sfodra kefalalghia.

dove sentite dolore adesso.

poo esthnesthe tora ponon.

ho dolore di testa.

ekho ponoos tis kefalis.

ho gran dolore di testa, mi sento che veglio vomitare.

ekho sfodran kefalalghian, ke m' erkhete na emese.

mi sento male allo stomaco.

esthanome ponoos ees ton stoma- khen.

ho mal di gola.

ekho ponolemon.

ho avuto il tremore tutta la nette.

eekha olin tin nikta righos piretoo.

ho dolore nel mio lato e non posse respirare.

ekho ponoos ees to plevron ke diskolevome n'anapevso.

come va il vostro appetito?

ekhete olighin orexin.

non ho mangiato guasi niente da due giorni.

apo dio imeron skhedon den efagha tipote.

mostratemi la vostra lingua.

na ido tin ghlossan sas.

la vostra lingua è un poco sporca.

i ghlossa sas den eene toson kathara.

sono umori nello stomaco.

ekhete akatharsian ees ton stoma- khen.

bisogna prendere un peco di me- dicina.

prepee na labete olighon iatrikon.

che toccho il vestro polso.

ithela na ido ton sfighmon sas.

il vestre polso è un peco agitato.

o sfighmos sas eene olighon dinatos.

il vostro polso è duro, vi è un pò di febbre.

o sfighmos sas ktipa barees, eene piretos.

voi avete un pò di febbre.

ekhete mikron pireton.

credete che la mia malatia è peri- celosa?

nomizete epikindinon tin asthe- neean moo.

no, ma badate che non divenga.

okhi, alla prosexate mi ghini epikindinos.

che cosa deve fare?

ti prepee lipen na kame.

vi manderó medicina da prendere, e verrò a vedervi domani matti- na.

tha sas steele kati na parete ke avrion proi sas blepo palin.

deve fare qualche altra cosa?

ekho ti allo na kame.

no, badate solamente di tenersi caldo.

okhi, frontisate menen na diatir- isthe thermos.

ENGLISH.	TURKISH.
Be careful not to catch cold.	sākin sòghuk àlmayasiniz.
How have you passed the night?	ghèjayi nàssl ghèchirdiniz.
How have you been since yesterday?	dùndanberi kìndinizi nàssl hiss idiyursiniz.
I feel much better.	kèndimi chòk àyi bòliyurim.
I have not been so restless, and I slept a little.	òl kàdar ràhātsiz dìghil idim vè bìr-àz ùydim.
The fever is much abated.	hàrārèt chòk kàfīflandi.
The fever is almost gone.	hàrārèt hàman ghìtti ghìbi dir.
Do you feel any more pain in your side, etc.?	shindi kàrninizda, yàminizda, hìch bìr vèjà hiss idiyùrmisiniz.
Much less than I did, I am a good deal easier.	èvvelki kàdar dìghildir bìr khàyli ràhātim vàr dir.
I will send you another bottle which you will take as you did yesterday.	siza bìr shìshè dàha ghyùnderirim dùnki ghìbi ìchiniz.
I can promise you that it will have no serious consequence.	shindi siza mùzhdè ìderim mùkhātarassi yòk dir.
In two or three days you will be quite well.	ìki ùch ghyùna kàdar bùtun bùtun àyi òlajaksin.

Chapter XXIX.

HIRED CARRIAGES.	KIRA "ARABALARA DA'IR.
Where are you going this morning?	bù sàbāh nèreya ghidajaksiniz.
I am going to make calls.	bìr kàch vìsita ìtmagha ghìdajaghim.
I have several calls to make.	èdà ìdajak bir khāyli visitalerim vàr.
I must go first to Mr.	èvvela fìlanin èvina ghìtmaim làzimdir.
You will not find him at home.	àni èvda bùlamazsiniz.
He is in the country.	kŗùya ghitti.
In that case I shall leave a card at his house.	bù sūrètta évina bìr kyāghid bràkarim.
Afterwards I shall go to see our friend B	àndan sòngra bìzim dòsstimiz fìlani ghyùrmagha ghiderim.

ITALIAN.	GREEK.
badate di non prendere freddo.	prosexate mi kriosete.
come avete passate la notte?	pos iperasate tin nikta.
come siete state da jeri fino ad oggi.	pos evriskesthe apo khthes.
mi sento molto meglio.	esthanome ton eavton moo poli kallitera.
non sono stato tanto agitato, e ho dormito un poco.	den imin toson erethismenos ke ekimithin olighon ti.
la febbre è molto diminuita.	o piretos poli olighostevsen.
la febbre è quasi sparita.	o piretos skhedon epavsen.
sentite più dolore ancora nei lati?	esthanesthe akemi ponoos ees to plevron.
molto meno, e mi sento molto meglio.	poli olighoteroos, esthanome ikanin elafrinsin.
vi manderò un altra botiglia, la prenderete come jeri.	tha sas steelo ke allin fialin, tin opian na metakheeristhite apos ke khthes.
vi prometto che non accaderà niente di sinistre.	diname na sas bebeoso, oti den tha eene spoodeon to praghma.
fra due o tre giorni sarete guarito.	ees dio i trees imeras tha ighianete.

CARROZZE D' AFFITTO.	PERI OXIMATO ME AGHOGHION.
dove andate questa mattina?	poo tha ipaghete tin proian tavtin.
vade a fare visite.	tha kame episkepsees.
ho molte visite a fare.	ekho diaforoos episkepsees na kamo.
devo prima andare dal Signore	prepee proton pros ton Kirie . . . na ipagho.
non lo troverete in casa.	den tha ton evrete en ti ikia.
egli è alla campagna.	eene ees tin exokhin.
allora lascerò il mi biglietto di visita a casa sua.	tote to afino entevxdion.
dope anderò a vedere il nostro amico . . .	isteron ipagho ees ton filon mas . . . . .

ENGLISH.	TURKISH.
Go there first, and I will accompany you.	ìptidā òraya ghìdiniz bènda siza àrkadash òlirim.
Let us go.	bùyurung ghìdalim.
Shall we ride or walk?	yàyanmi ghìdalim yòkhsa "àrabami tùtalim.
Let us ride, in order not to fatigue ourselves.	kìndimizi yòrmamak ìchin "àrabaila ghìdalim.
Just as you please.	nàssl isstersiniz ùylé idalim.
Let us look for a cab.	bìr kìrā "àrabassini ghyùz lèyalim.
We shall find a stand in the next street.	yàkindaki sòkaghin ichinda "àrabalarin dùrdighi bìr màhàll bùluriz.
Here is a cab, let us take it.	ìshta bìr "àraba bùni tùtalim.
I prefer taking a fly by the hour.	sā"atila bir "àraha tùtmassini terjīh ìderim.
Coachman, drive us to . . . . . Street.	"àrabaji fìlanja sòkagha bìzi ghìtir.
Set us down at No. 50.	nùméro èlli èvina bizi indir.
Here we are!	ìshta ghèldik.
Already!	né tèz!
Coachman, here is your fare.	"àrabaji ishta sènin hàkkin.
And here is something for yourself.	bùda sènin bàkhshishin.

IN AN OMNIBUS. — DOLMISH ARABASSIILA.

Motion to the driver to step.	"àrabajiya dùr dèyè ìshāret idiniz.
Call the conductor.	"àraba kàpijissini chàghirin.
There is no room.	"àrabada yèr yòkdir.
We are full.	mùshtèrīler tèkmìldir.
There is but one place.	yàliniz bìr kìshilik yèr vàr dir.
We must wait.	bèklemaliiz.
Here is another omnibus.	ishta bàshka dòlmish "àrabassi.
It does not go the same way.	bù òl-bìrinin ghìttighi màhàlla ghitmaz.
Conductor, where are you going?	èy kàpiji nèraya ghìdiyùrssin.
We are going to the Exchange.	bankaya ghìdiyùriz.
This is the omnibus we must take.	binajakimiz "àraba bù dir.

ITALIAN.	GREEK.
andate prima e vi accompagnerò.	ipaghete sees ekee proteron egho sas akolootho.
andiamo.	as ipaghomen.
anderemo montati o a piedi.	tha okhithomen i tha ipaghomen pezi.
montiamo in carrozza affinche non stancheremo.	as akhithomen dia na me apostasomen.
come vole.	opos thelete.
cerchiamo una carrozza.	as zitisomen okhima me aghoghion.
troveremo una nella strada vicina.	tha evromen ees tin prosekhi odon.
ecco una carrozza prendiamola.	idoo en okhima as to paromen.
preferisco d'avere una carrozza col' ora.	egho protimo amaxan me tin oran.
condottore conduceteci alla strada.	amaxilati, ipaghe mas ees tin odin.
portateci al numero 50.	ebghale mas ees ton arithmon 50.
eccoci, siamo arrivati.	idoo afthasamen.
cosi presto !	idi ; kiolas.
carrozziere ecce il vestro affitto.	amaxilati, idoo to aghoghion dia ton dromon soo.
ed ecco qualche cosa per voi.	na ke to kerasma soo.

IN UN OMNIBUS.	EES EN PANTOFOREEON.
fate segno al carrozziere di fermare.	kame simeron to amaxilati na stathi.
chiamate il carrozziere.	kraxe ton odighon.
non ce posto.	den eene topes.
tutti i posti sono pieni.	i amaxa eene ghemati.
non ce che un posto.	enas topos monen eene kenos.
bisogna che aspettiamo.	prepee na perimenite.
ecco un altro omnibus.	idoo alle pantoforeeon.
non va alla medesima parte.	alla ipaghee pros allin dievthinsin.
condutore, dove andate ?	odighe, poo ipaghete.
andiamo alla Borsa.	ipaghomen pros tin trapezan.
questo è l'omnibus che abbiamo a prendere.	tooto to pantoforeeon prepee na labomen.

ENGLISH.	TURKISH.
Let us get up.	bìnalim.
You get up first.	èvvela siz bininiz.
I cannot sit down.	òturameyurim.
Will you be so kind, Sir, as to sit a little farther on.	effendi kèrem idub bir-àz ùtèya ghìdarmisiniz.
Sit in this corner.	bù kùshaya òturin.
We are going very slowly.	pèk àghir ghìdiyuriz.
The street is crowded with carriages.	sòkak ''àraba tùludir.
We do not get on.	bìz ilerilamiyuriz.
When I am in a hurry I never get into an omnibus.	né wākit ''àjalé itmek issterissam bèn àssla bù dòlmish ''àraba-larina binmam.
Where are we now?	shindi biz nèrèyaiz.
We are in . . . Street.	fìlanja sòkakdaiz.
Conductor, let me down at the corner of . . . Street.	kàpiji bèni filanja sòkaghin ky-ùshéssinda indir.
Step, if you please.	kèrem idub dùriniz.
Let me get down first.	èvvela bèn inayim.
Take care.	ghyùzediniz.
Give me your hand.	èlini bàna vèr.
Take hold of my hand.	èlimi tùt.
Hold my arm.	kòlima dàyan.
Do not be in a hurry.	''àjélé itmeniz.

CHAPTER XXX.

BEFORE DEPARTURE.	YOLJULUK SUHBETTIDIR.
Have you any commission for London?	lòndra ìchin bir sìpārishniz vwarmi.
Are you going to London?	
Yes, is there anything I can do for you there?	èvet òraya bèndenizé hich bir sìpārishniz varmi.
You are very kind.	siz pek mùrùvvèt bùyur dunguz effendim.
When do you think of going?	né vaket ghitmeyeh mùlāhaza idiyursiniz.
I start to-morrow morning.	yarin sabah āzīmèt idejaghim.
Do you go by the stage coach?	mènzil ''àrabassilehmi ghidejak-siniz.

ITALIAN.	GREEK.
montiamo.	as anabomen.
montate voi prima.	anabite sees proton.
non posso sedere.	den eemboro na kathiso.
Signore, abbia la bontà di sedere un pò di là.	labete parakalo, Kirie, tin kalosinin na trabikhthite parekee.
sedete in questo cantene.	kathisate ees tavtin tin ghonian.
andiamo molto piano.	okhoometha poli argha.
la strada e piena di carrozze.	i odos eene pliris amaxon.
non avanziamo.	den prokhoroomen dioloo.
quando ho premura non vado mai coll' omnibus.	etan biaxome, pete den okhoome epi pantoforeeon.
dove siamo adesso.	poo eemetha tera.
siamo nella strada . . .	eemetha ees tin odon . . .
conduttore, discendetemi al cantone della strada di . . .	odighe, afes me na ebgho ees tavtin tin ghonian.
fermatevi se vi piace.	stathite, parakalo.
lasciatemi dicendere prima.	afes me na exeltho protes.
badate.	prosexte.
datemi la vestra mano.	dote mi tin kheora sas.
prendete la mia mano.	labete tin kheera moo.
tenete il mio braccio.	kratisate ton brakhiona moo.
non affrettatevi.	mi biazesthe..

PRIMA DELLA PARTENZA.   PRO TIS ANAKHORISEOS.

ha ella un qualche comande per Lendra e che? va ella a Lendra?	ekhete tina parangelian dia Londinon? aperkhesthe ees Londinon?
si, Signore, vé egli qual cosa ch'io pessa fare per lei?	né, deename ti ehhee na sas eepiretiso.
vossignoria è molto gentile.	eesthe polla kalos.
quando pensa partire?	pote stokhasesthe na anakhorisite?
parto domani mattina.	anakhoro avrion to takhi.
va nella diligenza?	eepaghete me tin kinin amaksan?

ENGLISH.	TURKISH.
I am going by train.	demiryòl àrabassileh ghidèjaghim.
How long shall you stay there?	òrada nàkadar èlenmèyé niyyitiniz vàr.
When shall you be back again?	né vākit "àvdet idèjaksiniz.
I think of staying four or five days.	dùrt bèshghyùn kàdar èylenmèk niyyèt ideyorim.
But I fear I may be detained longer.	kòrkarim bèlki zìyādéja kàlir.
It is very likely.	pèk ìhtimàldir.
Therefore it is better to reckon upon a longer time.	bù sèbebdan zìyādèja èlenmek ùzéré hìssāb ètmek òlader.
If I can be of any use to you there let me know?	ègher òrada sìzin bir ìshiniz zùhūr ider issa bana bìldìriniz.
I shall avail myself of your kind offer, and will call upon you in the course of the evening.	sìzin bù mùrùvvètlu tèklīfinizé kàbūl ìderim vè bù àkhsham zàrfindé sìzè ghèlùb ghyùru-rim.
You are sure to find me at home.	sìz bèni èlbètté èvdé bùlursiniz effendim.

TRAVELLING BY RAILWAY.   DEMIR YOL SUHBETTER.

Have you made all your preparations for departure?	"àzīmèt ìchin her bir tèdārekā-teniz ghyùrdùnizmi.
Everything is ready.	her shèy hāzirder.
Send for a porter to carry my luggage.	èshyāmi ghyùturmek ìchin bir hāmmāl chàghir.
I shall take the railway omnibus.	dèmir yelun "àrabassinè binarim.
Take that luggage to the omnibus office.	bù yùki "àraba màhàlliné ghètir.
We start in five minutes, Sir.	bèsh dàkīkayé kàdar kàlkajaghiz effendim.
Get up, if you please.	kèrem idùb bininiz effendim.
It seems to me to be very late.	bàna pèk ghèch ghyùriniur.
How soon shall we be at the station?	mèvkifa vwārmamiz nàkadar sùrer.
We shall be there in a quarter of an hour.	bir chār-yèk (chèyrek) zàrfinda òrada òlùruz.

ITALIAN.	GREEK.

vado per la strada ferata.

quando pensa restarci ?

quando sarà di ritorno ?

fo cento di starci quattro o cinque giorni.

ma temo esser ritenuto piu lungamente.

è cosa probabilissima.

però bisogna far capitale sopra un soggiorno piu lunge.

se posso servirla me lo dica.

mi gioverò dalla sua cortese offerta, e verrò da lei nella serata.

è sicuro di trovarmi in casa.

tha eepagho me ton sidirodromon.

pòson meletate na meenite ekee ?

póte tha epistrepsete ?

meleto na meeno ekee tessaras pente eemeras.

alla foboume mi empodistho perissoteron.

pòli pithanon tooto.

dia tooto eene kallion na ipothesite khronioteran tin diatribin sas.

an diname na sas khrisimevso ekee eepete moi to.

tha ofeliso tis prothimias sas ke tha eltho apopse ees imas.

na eesthe bebeos oti m'evriskete en ti īkia.

VIAGGIO NELLA STRADA FERRATA.

TAKSIDION EPI TON SIDIRODROMON.

ha fatto tutti i preparativi per la partenza ?

tutto e bello e pronto.

fate venire un facchino per portar via le robe mie.

piglierò l'omnibus della strada ferrata.

portate queste robe all' ufficio dell' omnibus.

partiamo fra cinque minuti, Signere.

menti in vettura, Signore.

mi sembra che sia molto tardi.

fra quante tempo saremo alla stazione ?

ci saramo fra un quarto d'ora.

pròetoimasthite kata panta dia tin anakhorisin ?

ta panta eene etoima.

às elthi ees bastaksos dia na metakhomisi ta praghmata mon.

tha labo thesin ees to pantoforeeon ton sidirodromon.

konbalisate tavta ta praghmata ees to grafeeon ton pantoforeeon.

meta pente lipta, Kirie, anakhoreumen.

anabite parakalo ees tas amaksas.

moi fenete oti eene poli arga.

ees posin oran tha eemetha ees ton stathmon tis embibasios ?

tha eemetha ekec sees en tetarton tis eras.

124 LEVANT INTERPRETER,

ENGLISH.	TURKISH.
I fear you will arrive too làte for the eight o'clock train.	kòrkarim dèmir yòlun sā"àt sèkiz "àrabàlariné yètishmèyejaksiniz.
Do not be uneasy, Sir, we are never too late.	tè "èssuf ètmeyeniz effindim biz àsslā ghèch kàlmaiz.
Here we are at the station.	ishté mèvkifa vwàrdik.
The train will start in five minutes.	demir yòl "àrabàlari bèsh dàkikayè kadar kàlkajakdir.
Make haste and take your ticket.	chàbik òl yòl kyāghidinizé àlùniz.
I will take a first-class seat.	birinji billiet issterim.
I will go in a second-class carriage.	ikinji fi'àt "àrabasiné binejaghim.
What luggage have you, Sir?	né yùkuniz vārdir effindim.
I have two trunks, a bag, and a hat box.	iki sāndùghim vār birdé chànta vé birdé kalpak kùtussu.
Take great care of the hat box.	chàpka kùtussuné bir īyijaghyùzèdiniz.
We have two engines.	bizim iki vàpor "àrabamiz òluyur.
It requires a strong power to draw a train of twenty-five carriages.	ighirmi besh "àrabaya chèkmek ichin chòk kùvvet lazimdir.
What is the power of these engines?	bù vàpor "àrabalerinin kùvveti nàkadir.
They are each of twenty horse power.	her birerleri ighirmi bārghīr (bèghir) kuvvetindédir.
Are we going by the fast train?	sùr"àtlu ghìdan "àrabalar ilèmi ghidejaghiz.
No, this is the slow train.	khàyr bù mèvkiflerde dùruji "àrabalardir.
At what o'clock does the goods train start?	yùk "àrabaleri sā"at kàchdé kàlkar.
There are two, one starts at ten in the morning, and the other at three in the afternoon.	her ghyùn iki dèf"à yùk "àrabalari vārdir biri sàbāhlèyin sā"at ondé òlbiri ùylindan sòngra ùchdé ghider.
It is a tunnel.	yèr àlti kèmer dir.
We are in the dark.	biz kàranlikda iz.
We shall soon be out of it, for the tunnel is not very long.	kèmer pèk ùzūn òlmadighindan bìz andan chabik kùrtaliriz.

ITALIAN.	GREEK.

teme non arrivate troppo tardi per il convoglio delle otto.

foboome mipos fthasete arga dia tin sinodian tin anakhoroosan kata tas okto.

non se ne pigli fasti-dio, Signore, arriviam sempre appunticio.

mi ekhete enneean, Kirie, imees den argoomen pete.

siam arrivati alla stazione ?

idoo ilthamen ees ton tathmon.

si partirà in cinque minuti.

e amakse anakhoroon entes pente lepton.

prende subito il vostro pighlietto.

parete ogligora to grammation sas.

prenderò il primo posto.

tha labo therin protis taksios.

prenderò il secondo posto.

ego tha eepago ees amaksan devteras takseos.

che bagaglio avete, Signore ?

tee prakhmata ekhete, Kirie ?

ho due bauli un sacco di viaggio ed una cappelliera.

ekho dio kibotia ena sakkon odiporikon ke mian thikin pilon.

badate bene la cappelliera.

epimeleesthe tis thikis ton kapellon.

abbiamo due machine a vapore.

ekhomen dio mikhanas.

bisogna una grande forsa per tirare convoglio di venticinque vetture.

khriaksete polla megali dinanis dia na seeri eekosipente amaksas.

di che ferza sono queste machine.

tis eene i dinamis teeton ton mikhanon ?

ciascuna è di ferza di venti cavalli.

pasa mia avton eene dinameos eekosi eeppon.

andiamo coll' espresso ?

tha ipaghomen kat' evtheean ?

no, questo è il traggitto colle fermate.

okhi, avti eene i kata stathmoos poria.

a che ora parte il convoglio delle merci ?

tee oran kinoon e amakse ton emporevmaton ?

ci sono due convogli che partono ogni giorno, uno parte alle dieci della mattina è l'altro alle tre depo mezzo giorno.

deeo seenodie tiooton amakson kinoon kath' imeran, i mia ees tas pro mesimbrias, i alli ees tas 3 pe. mesimbrian.

è un sotterraneo.

eene apogheeon orighma.

siamo nella tenebre.

eemetha ees to skotos.

adesso sortiremo presto, perché il sotterraneo non è molto lungo.

tha exelthomen met'oo poli, dioti to ipogheeon den eene pellis ektaseos.

ENGLISH.	TURKISH.
It seems to me, on the contrary, very long.	bi-l-"àks ò bàna pèk ùzūn ghyù- riniyur.
After this one we shall have to go through one of half a league in length.	bùndan sòngra ùzūnlighi yàrim mīllik yòl sùrur bàshka bìr kèmerdan ghèchejaghiz.
Here is another station ; are we to stop here ?	ìshta bìr mèvkif dàha, bùrada dòrajaghmiz.
Yes, we shall remain here five minutes.	èvvet, bùrada bèsh dàkika dòraja- ghiz.
Where are we now ?	shindi biz nèrédé iz.
It seems as if we were suspended in the air.	bàna hàwàda ùchiyuriz ghibi.
We are passing over a viaduct.	kèmer ùsstundan ghèchiyuriz.
Here is the last station but one.	bùndan sòngra yàliniz bìr ghèehe- jak mèvkif kàldi.
We have another bridge to pass over.	ghèchejaghimiz bír kyùpru dàha vàr.
We shall soon be at our journey's end.	bìz àzdan yòlimizi tèkmīl itmish òluriz.
This station is the last.	ìshta sòng mèvkif bù dir.
Will you give me your ticket, Sir.	kèrem idub tèzkérénizi bàna vèri- niz èffendim.
Here it is.	ìshta àl.
Let us go and get our luggage.	ghìdub yùkimizi àlalim.
Let us make haste to the omnibus, or we shall not get a place.	dòlmish "àrabasina yètishalim yòkhsa yèr bùlamaiz.
It seems to me that we are moving forward now with amazing swiftness.	bàna ghyùriniyùrki shindi bìz shàshlajak dèréjé sùr"àtila ìléri ghìdiyuriz.
I really begin to be frightened.	hàkīkàt kòrkmagha bàshladim.
I am afraid the engine will go off the rails.	vàpor "àrabassi yòlindan chìkar dèyé korkiyurim
Do not be afraid.	kàrkmaniz.
We are terribly shaken.	bìz pèk fèna sàrsaliyuriz.
It is because we are far from the engine.	vàpor "àrabasindan ùzàk òldighi- mizdan.

ITALIAN.	GREEK.
alcontrario mi pare che è molto lunge.	ex enantias ees eme fenete polla makron.
dopo questo avremo un altra mezo legga di lunghezza di traversare.	meta tooto tha ekhomen alle en imiseeas levghas.
ecco un altra stazione, fermeremo qui?	idoo ke allos stathmos, tha stamatisomen.
si, rimaneremo qui cinque minuti.	malista, tha stathomen edo pente lepta.
dove siamo adesso?	poo eemetha tora.
pare che noi siamo suspesi nell' aria.	ithele tis eepee oti eemetha ees ton aera apiorimeni.
ora passiamo sopra un ponte.	tora diabenomen epi enos odaghogheeoo.
questa è la penultima stazione.	idoo o protelevteos sathmos.
abbiamo un altro pente a passare.	ekhomen akemi mian ghefiran na perasomen.
fra peco arrivaremo alla fine del nostro viaggio.	entes olighoo tha eemetha ees to terma tis odiporias mas.
questa stazione è l'ultima.	o stathmos ootos eene o televteos.
datemi il vostro biglietto, Signore.	dote mi parakalo, Kirie, to eesitirion soo.
eccola.	idoo labete to.
andiamo a prendere il nostro bagaggio.	as ipaghomen na zitisomen ta praghmata mas.
andiamo presto all' omnibus altrimenti non troveremo pesto.	as spevsomen na fthasomen to pantoforeeon, allos den evriskomen topon.
pare che avvanziamo adesso con velocità incredibile.	mi fenete oti tin sighmin tavtin probenomen meta thavmasias takhititos.
davvero comincio di avere paura.	ti aletheea arkhiso na foboome.
teme che la macchina non sorte dalle guide.	foboome mi exelthi tis trokhias i mikhani.
non temente niente.	mi fobisthe tipote.
siamo terribilmente scossi.	klonizometha frikta.
la causa è perche siamo lontani dalla macchina.	i etia eene oti apekhomen makran tis mikhanis.

ENGLISH.	TURKISH.

There are twelve carriages, be-sides the tender, between ours and the engine.

bìzim "àrabamizila vàper "àra-bassi àrasinda kyùmur "àraba-sindan mā"àdā tàmām òn iki "àraba vàr.

Here is a train coming.

ìshta bìr "àraba sùrussi ghèliyur.

It is the up train.

ghèri ghìdan "àrabalar dir.

It looks as if it were on our line.

bizim yòlimizdan ghèliyur ghìbi ghyùruniyur.

Do not be alarmed, the up trains always go on the other line and the down trains on this one.

kòrkmaniz yùkāriya ghìdan "àra-balar dā'imā òl bìr yòldan àshàghiya ghìdanlar bù yòldan ghècher.

Here we are at the first station.

ìshta bìrinji mèvkifa ghèldik.

How long shall we stop here?

bùrada né kadar èyliyajaghiz.

We shall stop here only three minutes.

bùrada yàliniz ùch dàkika dòra-jaghiz.

There are a great many passengers waiting at the station.

mèvkifda khàyli yòljiler bèkliyur.

We are off again.

yèna ghìdiyuriz.

What do I see before us?

ìlérimizda ghyùrdighim nè dir.

Does your friend come with us?

dòsstiniz bizim ila ghèlejami dir.

No, he leaves at twelve o'clock by the ordinary train.

khàyr, ò sā"at òn ìkida kàlkan kàrishik "àrabalarila ghìdaja-dir.

Will he make a long stay at . . .?

fìlanja màhàllada chòk èylenejak-midir.

He will not remain there, he ex-pects to return to-morrow even-ing by the express train.

òrada èylenemayajakdir ò yàrin àksham àghir "àrabalarila "àv-det ìtmaya kòrkiyur.

Take your places, gentlemen.

effendiler yèrleriniza òturuniz.

Make haste, the train is just going to start.

chàbik òliniz "àrabalar hàmān (hèmèn) ghìtmek ùzerédir.

That is the signal for starting.

ìshta "àrabalarin kàlkajaghina ìshāretdir.

We are off.

ìshta ghìdiyuriz.

We have already gone four or five leagues.

biz shindidan dùrt bèsh sā"atlik yól àldik.

We have gone just six miles.

bìz tàmām àlti mīl ghìttik.

ITALIAN.	GREEK.
sono dodici carrozze oltre il tender, fra noi e la macchina.	eene dodeka amaxe ektos tis karboonapothikis, metaxi tis imeteras amaxis ke tis mikhanis.
ecco un convoglio che viene.	idoo erkhete mia sinedia.
è il convoglio del ritorno.	eene i tis epistrofis.
si vede come forse quasi sulla nostra via.	fenete oti eene epi tis imeteras odoo.
non avete paura, i convogli del ritorno sempre vanno sopra l'altra linea e i convogli delle partenze sopra questa.	mi tarattesthe e epistrefoose sinodie porevonte pantote epi tis allis ghrammis, ke e aperkhomene ekeese sinodie epi tavtis edo.
ecco siamo arrivati alla prima stazzione.	idoo efthasamen ees ton proton stathmon.
quante tempo fermeremo qui?	posen tha meenomen edo.
fermeremo qui solamente tre minuti.	okhi pleon ton trien lepton.
vi sono molti viaggiatori aspettano nella stazzione.	eene polli odipori perimenontes ees ton sathmon.
eccoci partiamo di nuovo.	idoo palin exekinisamen.
che cosa è questo che vedo innanzi a noi?	ti blebo embrosthen mas.
il vostro amico verrà con noi?	erkhete o files sas mazimas.
no, partirà alle dodeci col convoglio mischiato.	okhi, avtos anakhoree peri tin mesimbrian me tin miktin sinodian.
resterà molto tempo a . . . ?	tha diameeni poli ees . . .
non rimanerà la, ma ritornerà domani sera col convoglio di gran vitessa.	den tha mini eki, meleta na epanelthi avrion to esperas me tin bradian sinodian.
in vettura, Signori.	ees tas amaxas, Kiri-i.
fate presto il convoglio va partire immediatamente.	zpevsate i sinodia kence amesos.
ecco il segnale della partenza.	idoo to simeeon tis anakhoriseos.
eccoci partiti.	idi ekinisamen.
abbiamo di già fatto quatro o cinque leghe.	ekamamen tessaras i pente levghas.
abbiamo fatto appunto sei miglia.	ekamamen soza ex milia.

9

ENGLISH.	TURKISH.
We went the last mile in two minutes.	shindi ghèchdighimiz mīli ìki dàkikada àldik.
We go a mile and a half a minute.	dàkikada bìr bùchuk mīl gbìdiyuriz.
This is quick travelling.	pèk chàbik ghìdishdir.
The other day we were only two minutes and a half going a league.	ghèchen ghyùn bìr sā"atlik yòli ìki bùchuk dàkikada àldik.
Such speed would frighten me.	bù kadar sùr"àt bèni korkudir.
For my part I like going fast.	bènja sùr"àtli ghìtmaghi sèverim.
The faster we go the better I like it.	nèkadar chàbik ghìdabilir issa òl kàdar hàz ìderim.

Chapter XXXI.

EMBARKING.	GHEMIE BINMEK SUH-BETTIDIR.
When do you leave for France?	fèransayé né wàkit ghidéjaksiniz.
I shall leave in two days.	ìki ghyùné kadar ghidéjaghim.
Where do you embark?	nèrédan ghèmié binejaksiniz.
I intend to take the steamboat from London Bridge.	lònderé kyùprusindan vàpora binmeyé nìyyèt ìdiyurum.
Have you a passport?	yòl tèzkérénizi àldinizmi.
I went to get it this morning.	bù sàbah ani almagha ghittim.
I advise you to secure your place at once.	sìzè nàssīhàt ìdérim der "àkab ghidub yerinizi tùtuniz.
If you wait, perhaps you will not find a berth.	dàha beklersiniz bèlké yer bùlamaziniz.
Do you travel in the main cabin or the fore?	kìch kamarasindémi yòkhsa bàsh kamarasindémi ghyùdiyursiniz.
What is the price?	bàhaleri nassilder.
The first class is a guinea, and the second seventeen shillings.	birinji kamara ìghirmi bèsh vè ìkinji òn yèdi shilinder.
Let us take first class.	bìrinji kamara ila ghìdalim.
At what o'clock does the packet start?	ghèmi sā"at kàchde kalkajakdir.

ITALIAN.	GREEK.
abbiamo messo due minuti per fare l'ultimo miglio.	entos dio lepton dietrexamen to televteon milion.
facciamo un miglio e mezzo ogni minuto.	diatrekhomen en ke imisi milion to lepton.
questo è viaggiare velocissima-mente.	takhitati entos i poreea.
l'altro giorno eravamo due minuti e mezzo per fare una lega.	tes proalles dio ke imisi lepta monen na diadramomen mian levghan.
tale velocità mi fa paura.	tosavti takhitis me tromaxee.
intanto a me mi piace andare molte presto.	egho to kat' eme aghapo na taxi-devo oghlighora.
più presto che andiamo il più che mi piace.	osen takhitera porevometha toson perissoteron evkharistoome.

L'IMBARCO.

I EPIBIBASIS.

quando partite per la Francia?	pete anakhoreete dia tin gallian?
partirò in due giorni.	tha anakhoriso meta deea eemeras.
dove v' imbarcherete?	poo tha epibibasthite?
intendo di prendere il vapore dal pente di Lendra.	ekho scopon na embo ees to atmo-pleon to para tin ghefiran ton Londinon.
avete il passaporte?	ekhete to diabatirion sas?
son andate a prenderle questa mattina.	eepiga na to zitiso simeron proce.
vi consiglio di sicurare il vostro posto subbito.	sas simbolevo na ipaghite na pia-site ameses tin thesin sas.
se tarderete forse non troverete un posto.	an arghisite pleeoteron den tha evrete isos plion kitoniskon.
prenderete il primo ovvero il se-condo posto?	tha labete protin ee devteran the-sin?
quante è il prezzo dei posti?	peene eene e time ton thereon?
i primi è d'una ghinea ed i secondi di diciesette scellini.	e prote ekhann mian gheeeenea ke e devtere dekaepta selinea.
prendiamo i primi posti.	as labomen preta thesees.
a che ora parte il vappore?	tee oran kina to atmoploon?

ENGLISH.	TURKISH.
She leaves at four o'clock in the afternoon.	ùylandan songra sā"at dòrta kalkajakdir.
Where is your luggage?	sizin ìshyaniz nèrédédir.
I have sent it on to the wharf.	ìsskèléya ghyunderdim.
You are quite right.	chòk àyi ittiniz.
Have you been on board to secure your berth?	yèrinizi tùtmak ichin ghèmiya ghìttinizmi.
I have an excellent one.	pèk ràhātli bìr yèrim vàr.
That is well.	tàmām.
I always like to travel by night, for I gain a day by it.	bèn dà'imā dèngiza ghèyjé ghèchmek issterim.
How long are you generally crossing the Channel?	bòghazi ghèchmek èksèrìyyā né kàdar vwàkit chèker.
We are generally about twelve or fourteen hours from London Bridge to Boulogne.	èksèrìyyā lòndra kyùprusindan bùlona kadar òn ìkidan òn dùrt sā"at kadar chikar.
Lose no time, the vessel starts in half an hour.	vwàket ghètchirmaniz ghèmi yàrim sā"at kadar kàlkajakdir.
They are going to start.	shindi kàlkajakler.
I hear the bell.	chàngi ìshidiyurim.
Let us walk faster.	chàbikja yùruyalim.
The vessel might start without us.	ghèmi bèlki bizsizda kàlkar.
Here we are on board.	ishta biz shìndi ghèmida iz.
Go on shore, if you please, gentlemen, we leave directly.	èffendiler ìsskèléya chìkiniz bìz ìshta kàlkiyuriz.
Come, we must part.	ghèl èffendim chìrā yòk ayrmaliiz.
I wish you a pleasant voyage.	àllāh sèlāmet vèrsin.
Thank you.	èy wàllāh èffendim.
Write to me without delay.	bèndaniza dèr-"àkab mèktūb yāziniz.
Certainly.	èlbètté.
Where is my berth?	bènim yèrim nèrada dir.
Here it is, Sir, your name is written upon it.	ìshta èffendim bùrassi dir ìssminiz ùzérinda yàzilidir.
Be good enough to put my bag in my berth.	"ināyet ìdub bènim chàntamin yèrima kòyuniz.
We are off.	àrtik àyrildik.
Do you hear the noise of the engine?	màkinanin shàmatasini ishidiyurmisiniz.

ITALIAN.	GREEK.
partirà alle quatro depo mezzo giorno.	kina ees tas tessaras meta mesimbrian.
dove è il vostro bagaggio?	poo eene ta praghmata sas.
le ho già mandati al porto.	ta esteesla ees ton limena.
ha fatto molto bene.	ekamete poli kala.
siete stato a bordo per sicurare il vostro posto?	anebite ees to plion dia na piasite ton kitoniskon sas.
ne ho uno eccellente.	ekho ena polla kalon.
benissimo.	kalos.
mi piace sempre di viaggiare nella notte, e cosi guadagno una giernata.	aghapo pantote na diagho tin nikta ees tin thalassan dioti oote kardizo mian imeran.
in quanto tempo generalmente si fa il passaggio?	posen keron khreeazesthe sinithos dia ton diabloon.
si prende, generalmente, da dodici a quattordici ore circa per andare da Lendra a Boulogne.	kamnomen sinithos dedeka eos dekatessaras oras apo tis ghefiras too Londinoo mekhri Bononias.
non perdete tempo, il vapore partirà in una mezzo ora.	mi khanete keron, to plion anakhoree entes imiseeas eras.
si partirà fra peco.	th' anakhorisoon.
sento la campana.	akoo-o to koodooni.
camminiamo più presto.	as peripatisomen takhiteron.
il vapore forse partirà senza di noi.	eemboree to plion n' anakhorisi khoris imon.
eccoci siamo a bordo.	idoo epebibasthimen.
scendine a terra, Signori, dobbiamo partire subito.	Kirie, exelthete parakalo too plieo, dioti apopleomen ameses.
venga, dobbiamo separarsi.	lipon prepee na khoristhomen.
bon viaggio.	sas evkhome katevodion.
vi ringrazio.	sas evkharisto.
scrivetemi subito.	ghrapsate mi takheos.
senza dubbio.	bebeos.
dove è il mio posto?	poo eeneokitoniskos moo.
eccolo, Signore, il vostro nome è scritto sopra.	idoo avtos, Kirie, to onoma sas eene gheghrammenon ep' avtoo.
mettete vi pregho il mio baule nel mio posto.	balete, parakalo, ton odiporikon moo sakkon ees ton kitona moo.
ecce siamo partiti.	idoo ekinisamen.
sentite il romore della macchina?	akooete ton kroton tis mikhanis.

ENGLISH.	TURKISH.
It shakes the whole vessel.	bìtūn ghèmiyi sàrsiyur.
Let us go on deck.	ghyùghèrtéya chìkalìm.
Who is that standing on the paddle box?	dàwlumbāz ùsstunda dùran àdam kìmdir.
It is the captain, he goes up there to give his orders.	ghèminin kàptani nìdar kòmànda vèrmek ìchin òraya chìkàr.

CHAPTER XXXII.

DURING THE PASSAGE.	DENGNIZDA OLAN SOHPET DIR.
The tide is strong.	àkindi sèrt dir.
We are going rapidly.	pèk sùr"àtli gidiyuriz.
We shall not go so fast when we are in the open sea.	àchikda bù kàdar chàbik ghìtmaiz.
We are in smooth water here.	bìz bùrada līmànlikda iz.
We are now at the mouth of the Thames.	bìz shindi tāmìzin àghzinda iz.
The sea is rough.	dèngiz sèrt dir.
Are you going to hoist sail?	yèlken àchajakmisiniz.
No, the wind is against us.	khàyr, rùzghyar kàrshi dir.
So much the worse, we shall have a long passage.	yàzik, zīra ghèchmamiz ùzayajak dir.
I am going into the cabin, I do not feel quite comfortable.	kàmaraya ghìdiyurim kèndimi bìr-àz ràhàtsiz buliyurim.
What is the matter with you?	sìza né òldi.
I shall be sea-sick if I remain longer on deck.	ègher bìr-àz dàha ghyùghèrtéda dòrsam bèni dèngiz tùtajakdir.
For my part I am not subject to sea-sickness.	bèni àsslā dèngiz tùtmaz.
I wish I could say the same.	kèshké bènda sìzin ghibi dèyabilsam.
How have you passed the night?	ghyèjéi nàssl ghèchirdiniz.
Badly enough, the noise of the engine prevented my sleeping.	pèk fèna chàrk bèni ùykuya vàrmadan mèn" itti.
It is day-light.	sàbāh òliyur.
Where are we?	nérada iz.

ITALIAN.	GREEK.
fa tremare tutte il vapore.	kamnee na tremi olon to plion.
sortiamo alla coperta.	as ipaghomen ees to katastroma.
chi è questo uomo che è sul tamburo.	tis eene ootos o epi too emboloo.
è il capitano, monta là per dare gli ordini.	eene o pliarkhos, anabenee ekee dia na deni diataghas.

NEL PASSAGIO.

TA KATA TON DIAPLOON.

la marea è forte.	i apotholassia eene meghali.
andiamo rapidamente.	taxeedevomen oghlighora.
non anderemo tanto presto quando saremo in alto mare.	den th' armenizomen toson eghrighera otan embomen .ees to telaghos.
siamo nella calma qui.	i thalassa eene edo ghalinikia.
eccoci all' imboccatura del Tamigi.	idoo efthasamen ees tas ekbolas tis Tamisis.
il mare è tempestuoso.	i thalassa eene kimatodis.
alzerete le vele?	tha sikosete pania.
no, il vento è contrario.	okhi ekhomen enantion anemon.
peggio per noi, il traverso sarà lunge.	kala lipen, o diaploos tha eene makros.
vado alla camera, non mi sento bene.	egho katabeno kate, den esthanome toson kala ton evaton moo.
che cosa avete?	ti ekhete.
sofrirìò il mal di mare se resterò più lunge sulla coverta.	tha m' elthi navtiasis, an meeno pleeoteron epi too katastromatos.
io non sofro il mal di mare.	egho omes den ipokeeme ees tin navtiasin.
vorrei peter dire come voi.	ithela ke egho na idinamin na eepo to avto.
come avete passate la nette.	pos di-ilthete tin nikta.
un poco male, la macchina non mi ha lasciato dormire.	kamboson kaka, i mikhani den me afise na kimitho.
è fa giorno.	exeemeronee.
dove siamo?	poo eemetha.

ENGLISH.	TURKISH.
We shall soon be in sight of land.	yàkinda biz kàra ghyùrajakiz.
The sea is calmer.	dèngiz bìr-àz lìmānlidir.
The wind is not so high as it was.	rūzghyār òl kàdar sèrt dìghildir.
We are going very fast.	pèk sùr"àtli ghidiyuriz.
How many knots an hour are we going?	sā"àtta kàch mīl àliyuriz.
We will ask the helmsman.	dùmènjiya sù'āl idalim.
We are making ten knots an hour.	sā"àtta òn mīl ghidiyuriz.
We shall seen arrive.	yàkinda vàssil òluriz.
Here we are.	ìahta ghèldik.

CHAPTER XXXIII.

LANDING AND CUSTOM HOUSE.	KARAYA CHIKMAK VE GHYUMRUK.
Thank God, we have arrived safely.	hàkka shùkyurler òlssun sèlāme-tila ghèldik.
What o'clock is it?	sā"àt kàchdir.
It is eight o'clock.	sā"àt sèkis dir.
We have had a sixteen hours' passage.	tāmm òn àlti sā"àt yòl chikdi.
We cannot get into the harbour.	lìmana ghìramayajakhiz.
The tide is low.	dèngiz chèkilmishdir.
Gentlemen, you will be obliged to land in a boat.	èffendiler sàndalila kàraya chik-maz làzim ghèliyur.
The packet cannot enter the harbour for two hours.	ìki sā"àtta kàdar ghèmi lìmāna ghirmaz.
Here are the custom house officers.	ìshta ghyùmruk mè'mūrleri ghè-liyur.
Your luggage will be examined in about three hours.	yùkiniz ùch sā"àtta kàdar yòkla-najak dir.
This delay is very disagreeable.	bù kadar ghèch bràkmak dàdsizlik dir.
Will you return me my passport?	bènim tèzkèrémi ghiri vèr.

ITALIAN.	GREEK.
fra peco vedremo la terra.	entes olighoo tha eedomin tin aktin.
il mare è un poco calmo.	i thalassa eene pleon isikhos.
il vento è un poco più calmo.	o anemos eene astheneseros par' o, ti ito.
andiamo molto presto.	ipaghomen poli takheos.
quante miglia facciamo al ora?	posees kamboos kamnomen tin oran.
domandiamo al timoniere.	as erotisomen peri tootoo ton pidaliookhon.
facciamo dieci miglie all' ora.	kamnomen deka komboos tin oran.
arriveremo fra peco.	tha fthasomen ees olighon.
eccoci siamo arrivati.	idoo efthasamen.

Capitolo XXXIII.

LO SBARCO.	I APOBIBASIS.
grazie a Dio siamo arrivati sani.	dexa to Theo, idoo efthasamen ighiees.
che ora è?	ti ora eene.
sono le otto.	eene okto.
abbiamo messo seidici ore nel traverso.	ekamamen dekaex oras ees ton diaploon.
non possiamo entrare nel perto.	den dinamethe na embomen ees ton limena.
la marea è bassa.	i palirria eene tapeeni
Signori, sarete obligati di sbarcare nella barca.	Kiri-i, ananki na apobibosthite dia lemboo.
il vapore non può entrare nel perto prima di due ore.	to plion den tha dinithi na embi ees ton lemena eemi meta dio oras.
ecco i doganieri.	idoo i telone.
le vestre bauli saranno esaminati fra tre ore.	ta praghmata sas tha ta ideen entes trien eron.
questo ritardo è disagrievole.	avti i anaboli eene lian disarestos.
mi restituite il mio passaporto?	den tha mi desete opieo to diabatirion moo.

It will be returned to you in Constantinople, at the prefecture of police.

stàmbolda itissāb kàpisinda siza ghìri vèrelajak dir.

They will deliver you here a provisional passport, which must be backed by the English Consul.

bùradan siza dèghir mùwàkkàt bir tèzkèré vèrilir anida ìnghiliz kònsolossina imzā ittirmalisiniz.

All that is very tiresome, and causes great loss of time.

bùnlarin hèpssi dàdsizlik òldighindan mā"àdā àdama bìr khàyli wàkit zāyi" ittiriyur.

It is time to go to the Custom House for our things.

èshyāmiz ichin ghyùmruka ghìtma wàkti dir.

Will you please search this trunk at once ?

kèrem ìdub bù chàntaya dìr "àkīb yòklarmisiniz.

Take great care not to spoil anything.

dikkàt èt bìr-shèy bòzmayasiniz.

Now, tell me, do you know of a good hotel?

shindi bàna bàk hìch bìr ghyùzèl khàn bilirmisiniz.

Can you direct me to a good inn ?

bìr ghyùzél khàna bàna sàghlik vèrabilirmisiniz.

There are several very good ones.

bìr kàch tàna pèk ghyùzèl khanalar var dir.

Kindly direct me to the best.

kèrem idub bèni èn à"lassina sàghlik vèrin.

You may safely go to the Hotel d'Angleterre.

ingliz lòcandasina kòrkusinja ghidabilirsiniz.

You will find good accommodation.

òrada hèr bìr isstedighiniz bòlursiniz.

In which street is it ?

kànghi sòkakda dir.

I will take you there, if you like.

isstersaniz sizi òraya ghìteraim.

CHAPTER XXXIV.

IN AN HOTEL.

KHANADA OLAJAK SOHBET DIR.

See, gentlemen, this appears a good hotel.

èffendiler ishta òldikja ghyùsterishli bìr locanda.

Shall we alight here ?

bùnda inalimmi.

ITALIAN.	GREEK.
vi la daranno in Costantinopoli nell' offizzio della polizia.	thelee sas apodothi en Stimbolis en ti dievthinsee tis astinomias.
vi daranno qui uno provisionario il quale deve essere visé dal Console Inglese.	edo thelee sas dothi en prosonrinon diabatirion, to opien prepee na theorithi para too proxenoo tis Anghlios.
queste cese sono spiacevoli e fanno perdere molto tempo.	tavta panta eene lian disaresta, ke mas khasomeroon poli.
è tempo d'andare alla dogana per i nostri bauli.	eene keros naopaghomen ees to teloneenion pres zitisin ton praghmaton mas.
pregho di visitare questo baule subito.	exetasate parakalo evthis tooto to mbaoolon.
badate di non rovinare niente.	prosexate mi khalasete tipote.
vi pregho di dirmi, conoscete un buon hotel?	eepete mi tora, ghnorisete kanen kalon xenedokheeon.
potete diriggermi ad una buona locanda?	eemboreete na mi sisisite kanen kalon xenedokheeon.
vi sono varii buoni.	eene polla kala.
fatemi la gentilezza di diriggermi al migliore.	kamete mi tin kharin na me eepite to kalliteron.
può andare senza paura alla Locanda d'Inghilterra.	dinasthe na ipaghite en pasin asfaleea ees to xenodokheeon tis Anghlias.
li sarete molto comedo.	kala tha eesthe ekec.
in quale strada é?	ees pian odon eene.
se desidera vi condurrò li.	an epithimite sas odigho ekeese.

CAPITOLO XXXIV.

IN UN HOTEL.   EN XENODOKEEO.

ecce, Signori, una locanda di bell' aspetto.	Kiri-i, idoo xenodokeeon ekhon kalon exoterikon.
discenderemo qui?	kataliomen edo.

ENGLISH.	TURKISH.
Have you any spare rooms?	bòsh òdalarin vàrmi.
Can we sleep here?	bùraya yàtabilirmi iz.
Can you accommodate us for to-night?	bù ghèyjé bìza yàtak vèrabilirmisiniz.
Yes, gentlemen, you will find pleasant rooms and good beds here.	èvvet èffendiler bùrada hèm ghyùzèl òdalar vè hèmda ràhātli yàtak bòlursiniz.
You cannot find better beds anywhere.	bùradan à"là yàtak hich bàshka yerda bòlamazsiniz.
Above all, make a good fire, for we are very cold.	hepsindan mùkàddem bìr ghyùzél atesh yak zìra bìz sòghukdan dòngdik.
Waiter, show the gentlemen into the large parlour, and make a fire there at once.	ùshàk èffendileri bìyuk mùssāfir òdasina ghètir vè dèr-"àkab òrada àtesh yàk.
We shall do well to go and see if our horses have all they want.	èffendiler ghìdub ghyùralim àtlarimizi hèr bìr làzim yèrindami.
It is a good idea.	chòk ghyùzél mùlāhaza bùyùrdiniz.
Where is the estler?	ìsspir nèrada dir.
Here I am, gentlemen.	bùrada èffendiler.
Where are our horses?	àtlarimiz nérada dir.
They are in the stable.	àkhirda dir.
Have they eaten their oats?	yùlaflerini yèdilermi.
You have not been careful to rub them down as you ought.	ànlari dìkkàt ìdub ghyùzélja sìlmadin.
You have not washed their feet.	àyaklarini yèkamamishsin.
They are still covered with dirt.	ànlar dàha tàkmīl chàmur ichinda dir.
Wash them at once, and wipe them clean with straw.	dèr-"àkab ànlari yèka vè òtila tèmizja sìl.
Have you taken them to water?	ànlari sū-vèrmeya ghìtirdinmi.
Have you given them a drink?	ànlari sù vèrdinmi.
Give them a bundle of hay and some fresh straw.	ànlara bìr démet òt vè àltlarina bìr-àz tàzè sàp vèr.
To-morrow morning you will give them another feed of eats.	ànlara yàrin sàpāh bìr yèm dàha yùlaf vèrajaksin.
See whether their shoes are all right.	bàk nà"llari èyimidir.
Here is one which is very likely to give way on the road.	ìshta bìr tàmasi yòlda dùshmek ìhtimāli vàr.

avete camere libere ?
possiamo dormire qui ?
potete accomodarci questa notte ?

si, Signori, troverete qui belle
stanze e buoni letti.

non potete trovare altrove letti
migliori.
prima di tutto fateci un buon fuoco
perche siamo molto freddo.

cameriere conducete questi Signori
alla sala, e accendeteli subito
un buon fuoco.
andiamo a vedere se i nostri cavalli
hanno tutto l'occorente.
è un buen pensiere.

dove è lo stallone ?
eccomi, Signori.
dove sono i nostri cavalli ?
sono nella stalla.
hanno mangiato la loro biada ?
non gl' aveti nettato bene con un
poco di paglia.
non avete lavato i loro piedi.
sono ancora coperti di fango.

lavateli subito e sciugateli bene
cella paglia.
l' avete condotto a bevere ?
l' avete fatto bevere ?
dateli molto fieno e paglia fresca.

domani matina li darete ancora
una misura di biada.
guardate se i loro ferri sono bene.

ecco uno che forse caderà nella
strada.

ekhete kena domatia.
eemboroomen na kimithomen edo.
dinametha na katalisomen edo
avtin tin nikta.

malesta, Kiri-i, tha evrite edo
evmorfa domatia ke kalas
klinas.

poothena alloo den dinasthe na
evrite kalliteras klinas.
pro panton kamete mas kalin
fotian, dioti epaghosamen apo
tin psikhran.

pedi, odighise toes kirioos ees tin
meghalin ethoosan ke anapse
ekee fotian parevthis.
ipaghomen na idomen an i ippi
mas ekhoon ola ta khreeodi.
kala to estokhasthite.

poo eene o ippokomos.
edo ceme, Kiri-i.
poo eene ta alogha mas.
eene ees ton stavlon.
efaghan tin bromin.
den tripsite kathes prepee me
akhiron.
den eplinate ta podaria ton.
eene akemi olos leromena.

plinete ta parevthis, ke tripsate ta
kala me akhiron.
ta epighete ees to potistirion.
ta epotisate.
dote ta en dema khortoo ke nopon
akhiron.

avrion to takhi na ta desete akomi
en metron bremis.
idete an ine kala ola ta petala ton.

idoo en, to apion eemboree na
khathi ees ton dromon.

ENGLISH.	TURKISH.

Take my horse to the farrier, and have another shoe put on immediately.

bènim àti nà"lbanda ghìtùr bìr yèni nà"l chàksin.

CHAPTER XXXV.

WITH AN HOTEL KEEPER.

LOKANDAJI ILA SOHPET DIR.

Gentlemen, what do you wish to have for your supper?

What have you to give us?

I have a leg of mutton, a duck pie, and some cold fowl.

Or, if you prefer it, I will order some pigeons to be roasted.

Choose what you will like best.

Bring in a good cold fowl, and the pie.

Above all, let us have some of your best wine.

Do you want anything else?

No, only let us have our supper quickly, for we want to rest ourselves.

You shall be served in a minute.

Are our portmanteaus in our rooms?

Yes, gentlemen, I had them carried up before me.

Are our rooms ready?

Are the beds ready?

Are you sure the sheets are well aired?

I am going to bed, and will endeavour to sleep.

I advise you to do the same.

Waiter, remember that we want to set out exactly at six o'clock.

èffendiler ghèyjé tà"àminiz ìchin né ìsstersiniz.

bìza vèrajak né niz vàr.

bìr kòyun bùti bìr ùrdek bùreki vè bìr àzda sòghuk tàwuk vàr.

ègher tèrjìh ìdèrsiniz bìr kàch ghyùghèrjin kìzarttìrayim.

hèr né zìyadé sèversiniz ìntikhāb idiniz.

bìr ghyùzèl sòghuk tàwuk ila ùrdek bùrekini ghitir.

hèpsindan èvvel èn à"là sharabindan bìr-àz ghìtir.

dàha bàshka bìr shèy ìsstermisiniz.

khàyr, fàkat tà"àmimizi chàbik ghìtir zìra bìz dìnglenmek ìssteriz.

bìr dàkikaya kàdar hàzir òlur.

chàntalarimiz òdamizdami dir.

èvvet èffendiler ànlari ghyùzim ùnunda yòkari ghìttirdim.

òdalarimiz hàzirmi dir.

yàtakler yàpildimi.

chàrshaflerìn yòkila kùrumish òldighini èyī bìlirmisiǹ.

yàtmagha ghìdiyùrim ùyumagha sà"i iderim.

sizada bùyléja nàssīhàt iderim.

ùshak khàtirinizda òlsin bìz yàrin sà"àt àltida yòla chikajaghiz.

ITALIAN.	GREEK.
portate il mio cavallo al ferriere di ferrarlo di nuovo.	ipaghete to aloghon moo ees ton petalan, na to petalosi palin parevthis.

CAPITOLO XXXV.

COLL' ALBERGATORE.	META XENODOKHOO.
Signori, che cosa disederate per la vestra cena?	Kiri-i, ti aghapate dia to deepnon sas.
che cosa avete a darci?	ti ekhete na mas dosite.
ho una coscia di mottone, un pasticcio d'anitra a gallina freddo.	ekho en mirion probatoo, mian pittan me papies, ke poolerika kria.
oppure, se preferite farò arrostire alcuni piggioni.	i an prokrinete na balo peristeria ees ton obelon.
scegliete quel che vi piacerà di più.	eklexate o ti aghapate kallitera.
portateci del buon pollame freddo ed il pasticcio.	ferete mas kala poolerika kria ke tin pittan me papian.
dateci, specialmente, il miglior vino che avete.	pro panton de dote mas apo ton ariston sas inen.
volete qualche altra cosa?	den thelete allo tipote.
no, ma portateci la cena presto perché vogliamo riposare come siamo stanchi.	okhi, menen na ghini i etimasia takheos, dioti ekhomen ananghin anapavseos.
saranno serviti in un memento.	tha sas ipiretisomen ameses.
le bauli sono nelle nostre camere?	eene ta kibotia mas entos ton demation mas.
si, Signori, vi le ho fatto portare.	malista, Kiri-i, epi paroosia moo ebala ke ta ekoobalisan.
le nostre camere sono pronti?	eene etima ta domatia mas.
sono fatti i letti?	e kline eene dievthetimene.
siete sicuro che le lenzuole sono ben sciugati?	eesthe bebeos, an eene steghna ta sindonia.
vade al lette e cerco di dormire.	tha plaghiaso ke tha prospathiso na kimitho.
vi consiglio di fare lo stesso.	sas simboolevo na kamite to avto.
cameriere, ricordatevi che vegliamo partire alle ore sei precise.	pedi, enthimoo oti thelomen na kinisomen ees tas ex akribos.

ENGLISH.	TURKISH.
I shall take care to come and wake you.	sizi ghèlib ùyandìrmagha dikkàt iderim.
Where is your master?	sanin àghan nèrada dir.
We wish to settle with him.	bìz aninila hèsapimiz ghyurmek issteriz.
He is just coming.	ìshta ghèliyur.
How much do we owe you?	siza bòrjimiz né dir.
Have you made out our bill?	bizim hèssapimizi hàzirladinmi.
How much does our bill come to?	bizim hèssapimiz kàcha bāligh òlìyur.
It is . . . . for your supper and beds, and . . . for your horses.	shù kàdar ghèyjé tà''āmila yàta-ghiniz ichin vè shù kàdar àtla-riniz ìchin.
It is a great deal, but we must submit to it.	pèk chòkdir àmma bìz àna ràzi òlmali iz.

Chapter XXXVI.

<table>
<tr><td>EN ROUTE.</td><td>YOLDA DIR.</td></tr>
</table>

Are you going to Smyrna?	izmirami ghidiyùrsiniz.
Do you go all the way to Alexandria?	tā ìsskenderiya kàdar ghidiyurmi-siniz.
I do, Sir.	èvvet èffendim.
Then I shall have the pleasure of your company, for I am going there myself.	bù sūrètta siza bìlmìmnūniyyèt àrkadash òlorim zira bènda òraya ghìdiyurim.
I am very glad of it.	bèndanizda àndan ziadéssila hàz ittim.
Company makes a journey seem shorter.	sòhpetla yòl ghitmek kìssa ghyù-runiyur.
It is very disagreeable to travel alone.	yàliniz sèyāhàt itmek pèk lezzét-siz.
But together, we can talk and time passes quickly.	làkin arkadashla kòshàrak sùwey-larek wàktin hiss òlinmaz.
How far do they calculate from here to Smyrna?	bùradan ìzmira nàkadar yòl sày-arlar.
They call it seventy leagues, but it is less.	yètmish sā''àtlik yòldir diyurler àmma sā''àtleri kissa dir.

ITALIAN.	GREEK.

avrò cura di venire a svegliarvi.

dove è il vostro padrone?

vogliamo pagare il nostro cento.

eccolo che viene.

quante vi dobbiamo?

avete fatto il nostro cento.

quante è il nostro cento?

mi debbono . . . per la loro cena eper il loro lette e . . . pei loro cavalli . . .

è molto, ma siamo obligati a summettere.

tha frontiso na eltho na sas exipniso.

poo eene o kiries soo.

thelomen na idomen ton loghariasmon mazi too.

idoo erkhete.

posa sas khreostoomen.

ekamete ton loghariasmon mas.

posen anabenee o loghariasmos mas.

. . . dia to deepnon ke tin klinin ke . . . dia t' alogha sas.

eene polla, alla ipomoni.

CAPITOLO XXXVI.

IN VIAGGIO.

TA KATA TIN ODIPORIAN.

ella va a Smirne?

ella va fino ad Alessandria.

si, Signore.

avrò dunque il piacere della vostra compagnia anche io vade fino la.

mi sono veramente contento.

la compagnia fa parere meno lunga la strada.

è gran neia di viaggiare solo.

ma quando si è in compagnia il tempo passa col conversazione.

quante miglia si contano di qui fino a Smirne?

si contano settanta miglia ma sono meno.

ipaghete ees Smirnoos.

tha ipaghete eos ees toos Alexandrioos.

malista, Kirie.

tha ekho lipon tin evkharistisin too na sintaxeedevso mazi sas, dioti ke eghó ekee ipagho.

khero akros.

i sintrofia kamnee ton dromon sintomon.

eene poli disareston na taxeedevi tis mones.

all' otan eene sintrofia sinomeeli tis, ke o keros perna khoris na to ennoisi.

poson eene ap' edo eos Smirnioos.

arithmoosin ebdomikonta eevgha, all' eene brakhee-e.

10

ENGLISH.	TURKISH.

When do you think we shall reach Smyrna?

izmira né wàkit wāssil òluriz zan idersiniz.

I hope we shall arrive to-morrow.

in-shā-'llāh yàrin wāssil òluriz.

But it may be rather late.

bèlki bir-àz ghèch yètishiriz.

The roads are heavy.

yòllar èyī dìghildir.

The rain has spoiled the roads.

ràhmet bùtun yòllari bòzdi.

Did you ever travel this way before?

bù yòldan mùkàddem ghèchtinizmi.

Several times.

bìr kàch dèf"à.

I know the road perfectly well.

bù yòli pèk à"la bilirim.

Where is the first stage?

bìrinji mènzilkhané nèrédédir.

Where do they change horses?

àtlari nèrédé dìghishdirajaklar.

Shall we not pass through . . . ?

fìlanja màhàlldan ghèchmayajak-mi iz.

No, we leāve it on our left.

khàyr, àni sòlimizda bràkiriz.

But we shall pass through . . . , where they step to change horses.

lākin fìlanja màhàlldan ghècheja-ghiz òrada dòrub àtlari dighish-dirirler.

Where shall we sleep?

nèrédé yàtajaghiz.

We shall sleep at . . . , from which place there are only sixteen posts to Chianakala.

fìlanja màhàlda ghèyjéyi ghèchir-ajaghiz òradan chàna kàyléya fàkat òn àlti pòrta kàlir.

Then we shall be more than half way.

òl zàman yàri yòldan zìyādésini ghìtmish òloriz.

Yes, but then there are many hills, and the roads are generally very bad.

èvvet àmma daha bìr khàyli tèpè-ler vàr ve yòllar èksèrìyyā pèk fèna dir.

Why, then, do they prefer this road to the other?

bù sūrètta nichiu bù yoli òl bìr yòla tèrjīh idiyurlar.

Because they save two posts.

zìra iki pòsta kyārleri vàr.

That is important, for travelling is very expensive.

àz shèy dìghildir chùnki sèyāhàt ìtmek pèk màssraflidir.

For my part, I am very glad of your company.

bènja àrkadashlighinizdan pèk mèmnūnim.

But I confess I wish we were there.

lākin dòghrussi bènja kèshké shindi wāssil òlaidik.

I quite believe you.

siza pèk à"la inanirim.

Let us have patience.

lākin sàbr idalim.

A few hours more, and we shall be at our journey's end.

bìr kàch sā"àta kàdar yòlimiz tèkmīl òlur.

ITALIAN.	GREEK.
quando pensate che arriveremo a Smirne.	pete nomisete, tha fthasomen ees Smirnoos.
spero che arriveremo domani.	elpiso na fthasomen avrion.
ma forse sarà tardi.	all' isos fthasomen orgha.
le strade sono faticose.	e odi eene diskoli.
la pioggia ha rovinato le strade.	i brokhi ekhalasen tas edoes.
avete viaggiato di qui prima?	ekhete idi kamee tavtin tin odon.
molte volte.	polles fores.
conosco la strada molto bene.	ghnoriso kallista tin odon tavtin.
dove è la prima posta?	poo eene o protos stathmos.
dove cambiano i cavalli?	poo allazoon toes ippoos.
non passeremo per . .	den diabenomen dia . . .
no, lo lasciamo a sinistra.	okhi, t' afinomen aristera.
ma passeremo per . . . dove cambiano i cavalli.	alla tha diabomen dia . . . opoo stamatoomen dia n'allaxoon toos ippoos.
deve dormiremo?	poo tha kimithomen.
dormiremo a . . . e di la non avremo che sedici poste per arrivare ai Dardanelli.	tha kimithomen ees . . . ke ap' ekee den ekhomen pleon para dekaex stathmoos dia na fthasomen ees chanakalle.
allora avremo la metà della strada a fare.	tha eemetha lipen idi pleon too imiseos dromoo.
si, ma vi sono molti menti e le strade sono tutti cattivi.	ne, alla eene parembros ke polli lofi, e de odi eene katholoo copeen polla kake.
perché allora preferiscano questa strada all' altra?	dia ti lipòn protimosi tavtin tin odòn para tin allin.
perchè si guadagna due poste.	epeedi kerdenee tis dio stathmoos.
questo è importante, perchè per viaggiare costa caro.	tooto den eene axiokatafronitoo, dioti i idiporia kathistate polla akribi.
intanto a me ho molto piacere della vestra compagnia.	to kat' eme, lian evkharistoome na apolavo tis sintrofias sas.
ma vi dico la verità che vorei essere già arrivate.	all' egho sas omologho, oti ethela na eeme idi fthasmenos.
vi credo.	sas pistevo.
abbiamo un pò di pazienza.	all' ipomoni.
peche ore ancora e saremo alla fine del viaggio.	akemi olighas oras ke tha eemetha ees to terma tis odiporias mas.

CHAPTER XXXVII.

THE LORD'S PRAYER.   SALAT RABBANI.

Our Father which art in heaven, hallowed be Thy name. Thy kingdom come. Thy will be done in earth, as it is in heaven. Give us this day our daily bread. And forgive us our trespasses, as we forgive them that trespass against us. And lead us not into temptation ; but deliver us from evil: for thine is the kingdom, the power, and the glory, for ever and ever. Amen.

èy ghyūklerda òlan pèderimiz ìssmin mùkàddèss òlsun mèlé-kyūtin ghelsin mùrādin ghyūk-da nījé kilinir-issa yèrda dàkhi bùylé kìlinsin her ghyùnki èkmckimizi bùghyùn bìza vèr vè bìza sùchlarimizi bàghishla nījéki bìz dàkhi bìza sùchli òlanlara bàghishlariz vè bizi ìghwāya sàllama àmmā bìzi shèrīrdan kùrtar chūn mèlékyūt vè kùvvet vè "ìzzet èbéden sènindir. āmīn.

CHAPTER XXXVIII.

THE PARABLE OF THE   EKIJININ MISSALI.
        SOWER.

And He taught them many things in parables, and said unto them in His doctrine: Hearken ; behold, there went out a sower to sow : and it came to pass, as he sowed, some fell by the way side, and the fowls of the air came and devoured it up. And some fell on stony ground, where it had not much earth ; and immediately it sprang up, because it had no depth of earth : but when the sun was up, it was scorched ; and because it had no root, it withered away. And some fell among thorns, and the thorns grew up,

tèmsīllerila ànlara chòk shèyler tà"lim idub tà"līminda ànlara dèdiki. dìngléniz ìshta èkiji èkin ekmagha chikdi. vè vwāki" òldiki èker èken bà"-zissi yòl kènārina dùshmekla (hàwa) kùshlari ghèlub àni yèdi. vè bà"zissi chòk tòp-raghi òlmayan tàshligha dùshub tòpraghin dèrinliki òlmadigh-indan tèz bìtti issada. ghyù-nèsh dòghdikda yàndi vè kyùki òlmadighindan kùrudi. vè bà"zissi dìkena àrassina dùshmekla dìkenlar chìkib àni bòghdiklari ichin màhsūl vèr-madi. vè bà"zissi àyi tòpragha

PADRE NOSTRO.

padre nostro, che sei nei cieli, sia santificato il tuo nome. il tuo regno venga. la tua velentà sia fatta in terra come in cielo. dacci oggi il nostro pane cotidiano. e rimetteci i nostri debiti, come noi ancora li rimettiamo ai nostri debitori. e non indurci in tentazione, ma liberaci dal male : perciocchè tuo è il regno, e la potenza, e la gloria, in sempiterno. amen.

PATER IMON.

pater imon o en tis ooranis, aghiasthito to onoma soo. eltheto i basileea soo. ghenithito to thelima soo, os en oorano, ke api tis ghis. ton arten imon ton epioosion dos imin simeron, ke afes imin ta ofeelimata imon, os ke imees afiemen tis ofeeletes imon, ke mi eesenenkis imas ees peerasmon, alla rise imas apo too poniroo, oti soo estin i basileea ke i dinamis ke i doxa ees toos eonas. amin.

LA PARABOLA DEL SEMINATORE.

ed egli insegnava loro molte cese in parabole, e diceva loro nella sua dottrina : udite : ecce, un seminatore usci a seminare. ed avvenne che, mentre egli seminava, una parte cadde lunge la via, e gli uccelli vennero, e la magiarono. ed un' altra cadde luoghi pietrosi, ove non avea melta terra ; e subito nacque, perciocchè non avea terreno profondo ; ma, quando il sole fu levato, fu riarsa : e, perciocchè non avea radice, si seccó. ed un' altra cadde fra le spine, e le spine crebbero, e l'affogarono, e non fece frutto.

PARABOLIS O SPEERON.

ke edidasken avtoos en paraboles polla, ke eleghen avtis en ti didakhi avtoo, akooete, idoo, exilthen o speeren too speere, ke egheneto en to speereen, o men epese para tin odon, ke ilthe ta peteena too ooranoo ke katefaghen avto. allo de epesen epi to petrodes, opoo ook eekhe ghin pollin ke evtheos exaneteele, dia to mi ekheen bathos ghis ilioo de anateelantos ekavmatisthi, ke dia to mi ekheen rizan exeranthi. ke allo epesen ees tas akanthas ke anabisan e akanthe, ke sinepnixan avto, ke karpen

ENGLISH.	TURKISH.

and choked it, and it yielded
no fruit. And other fell on
good ground, and did yield
fruit that sprang up and in-
creased ; and brought forth,
some thirty, and some sixty,
and some an hundred. And He
said unto them, He that hath
ears to hear, let him hear.

dùshmekla chìkib bìyudikda
bàshak vèrarek kimi ùtūz
kimi àltmish vè kimi dàkhi
yūz kàt màhsūl ghìtirdi. vè
ànlara ìshidir kòlaklari òlan
ìshitsin dèdi.

CHAPTER XXXIX.

PARABLE OF THE GOOD SAMARITAN.

IYE SAMERIYALININ NINSAH.

A certain man went down from
Jerusalem to Jericho, and fell
among thieves, which stripped
him of his raiment and wounded
him, and departed, leaving him
half dead. And by chance there
came down a certain priest that
way: and when he saw him he
passed by on the other side.
And likewise a Levite, when he
was at the place, came and
looked on him, and passed by on
the other side. But a certain
Samaritan, as he journeyed,
came where he was: and when
he saw him, he had compassion
on him. And went to him, and
bound up his wounds, pouring
in oil and wine, and set him on
his own beast, and brought him
to an inn, and took care of him.
And on the morrow when he
departed, he took out two pence,
and gave them to the host, and
said unto him, Take care of

bìr àdem ùrashlimda àrihyaya
ìner ìken hàrāmiler èlina
dùshdi vè ànlar àni sòyib yàra-
ladikdan sòngra yèri ùlmish
bràghib ghìttiler. vè ìttifākā
òl yòldan bìr kyābin ìner ìken
àni ghyùrdikda òl-bìr tàrafdan
ghèchib ghìtti. kèzālik òl
màhàlla bìr làvili dàkhi ghèl-
mekla vàrib àni ghyùrinja òl-
bìr tàrafdan ghèchib ghìtti.
lākin bìr samariyali yòla ghìdar
ìken bùlindighi yèra ghèlib
àni ghyùrdikda tèràhhum itti.
vè yànina ghèlib yàralarina
zèyt yàghi ila shàrab dùkarek
ànlari sàrdi vè àni kèndi hày-
wānina bìndirarek bìr khāné
ghitirib àna mùkàyyèd òldi.
vè èrtéssi ghyùn yòla ghìtmek
ùzere-iken iki dinār chìkarib
khānjiya vèrerek bùna mùkàyyèd òl vè ziyādé hèr né khàrj
ider issan bèn tèkrer ghèldi-
ghimda sàna èdā iderim dèdi.

ITALIAN.

ed un' altra cadde in buona terra, e portò frutto, il quale montò, e crebbe : e portò, l'un trenta, l'altro sessanta, e l'altra cento. poi egli disse, chi ha orecchie da udire, oda.

GREEK.

ook edoke. ke alle epèsen ees tin ghin kalin ke edidoo karpen anabenonta ke avxanonta, ke eferen en triakonta, ke en exikonta, ke en ekaton. ke eleghen avtis, o ekhon ota akooeen akooeto.

LA PAROBOLA DEL BUON SAMARITANO.

PARABOLIS TIS ZAMAREE-TIS.

e Gesù disse, un uomo scendeva di Gerusalemme in Irico, e s'abbatté in ladroni : iquali, spogliatolo, ed anche dategli di molte ferite, se n'andarono, lasciandolo mezzo morto. or a caso un sacerdote scendeva per quella stessa via : e, veduto colui, passò oltre di rincontro. simigliantemente ancora, un Levita, essendo venuto presso di quel luogo, e vedutolo, passò oltre di rincontro. ma un Samaritane, facendo viaggio, venne presso di lui : e, vedutolo n'ebbe pietà ; ed accostatosi fasciò le sue piaghe, versandovi sopra dell' olio, e del vino ; poi lo mise sopra la sua propria cavalcatura, e lo menò in un albergo, e si preso cura di lui. ed il giorno appresso, ò partendo, trasse fuori due denari, e li diede all' oste, e gli disse. prenditi cura di costui ; e tutte ciò

o Iisoos eepen, anthropos tis katebenen apo Ieroosalim ees Ierikho, ke listes periepesen, i ke ekdisantes avton, ke plighas epithentes apilthon, afentes imithani tinkhanonta. kata sinkirian de ierevs tis katebenen en ti odo ekeeni, ke idon avton antiparilthen, Zamareetis de tis odevon isthe kat' avton, ke idon avton esplankhnisthi ke proselthon katedise ta travmata avtoo, epikheon eleen ke inon epibibasas de avton epi to idion ktinos, ighaghen avton ees pandokeeon, ke epemelithi avtoo, ke epi tin avrion exelthon, ekbalon, dio dinaria edeke to pandokhee, ke eepen avto, epimelithiti avtoo ke o ti an prosdapanisis, egho en to epanerkhesthe me apodoso si. tis oon teeton ton trien dokee si plision gheghonene too embesontos ees too listas ; o de

him ; and whatsoever thou spendest more, when I come again, I will repay thee. Which now of these three, thinkest thou, was neighbour unto him that fell among the thieves? And he said, He that shewed mercy on him. Then said Jesus unto him, Go, and do thou likewise.

ìmdi sàna bù ùchdan kànghissi hàrāmilerin èlina dùshanin kòngshussi (komshussi) òlmish ghyùruniyur. òld dàkhi àna mèrhàmet idan dedi. "'īssà dàkhi àna ghìt sènda bùila yàp dèdi.

CHAPTER XL.

TEXTS.

METNLER.

There is one God and one Mediator between God and men, the man Christ Jesus.—1 Tim. ii. 5.

zìra bìr Allāh vàr vè bìr àllāhin và ādemlerin àrassinda bìr mì-yānji vàr bù dàkhi ìnsān òlan mèssīh "'īssà dir. — tìmùtaus bìrinji rèssalassi.

Behold, now is the accepted time! behold, now is the day of salvation.—2 Corinthians vi. 2.

ìshta shindi màkbūl wàkit, ìshta shindi khàlāsi ghyùnidir. — korintius, àltinji bāb.

Jesus said, I am the way, and the truth, and the life; no man cometh unto the Father, but by me.—John xiv. 6.

"'īssà dèdi àna tàrīk vè hàkīkàt ve hàyāt bèn im, bèn vwāssita òlmadikja pèdera kìmsé ghèlemaz.—yàhyanin ìnjīli.

Believe on the Lord Jesus Christ, and thou shalt be saved, and thy house.—Acts xvi. 31.

ànlar dàkhi ràbb "'īssā il-mèssīh īmān ghètir vè kèndin vè èhli-bèytin khàlāss bòlajaksiniz dèdi.—à"māl rèssūller xvi. 31.

The blood of Jesus Christ, His Son, cleanseth us from all sin. —1 John i. 7.

vè ànin òghli "'īssà el-mèssīhinin kàni bìzi hèr ghyùnāhdan tàthīr ider.—yùhanna rèssūlin rissalassi i. bābb i. 7.

Behold the Lamb of God! which taketh away the sin of the world.—John i. 29.

ìshta dùnyānin ghyùnāhini rèf'' idan Allāhin kùzussi. — injīl yùhānnanin i. bābb. 29.

che spenderai di più, io tel renderò quando io ritornerò. quale adunque di questi tre ti pare essere stato il prossimo di colui che s'abbattè nei ladroni? ed egli disse, colui che usò misericordia inverso lui. Gesù adunque gli disse, và, e fà tu il simigliante.

eepen, "o pi-isas to eleos met' avtoo." eepen oon avto o Iisoos, "porevoo, ke si piee omios."

TESTI.

v'è un sol Dio, ed anche un sol mediatore di Dio e degli uomini Cristo Gesù uomo.—1 Epistola a Timoteo ii. 5.

ees ghar Theos, ees ke mesitis Theoo ke anthropon, anthropos Khristos Iisoos.—1 pres Timotheon ii. 5.

ecco ora il tempo accettevole, ecce ora il giorno della salute.— 2 Cor. vi. 2.

idoo nin keros evprosdektos, idoo nin imera sotirias. — 2 pros Korinthioos vi. 2.

Gesù gli disse, Io son la via, la verità, e la vita; niuno viene al padre se non per me.—San Giovanni xiv. 6.

leghi avto o I-isoos, eghò eemi i odos ke i alitheea ke i zoi, oodees erkhete pres ton patera, ee mi di' emoo.—Evanghelion kata Ioannin xiv. 6.

credi nel Signor Gesù Criste, e sarai salvato tu, e la casa tua.— Fatti xvi. 31.

pistevson epi ton Kirien I-isoon Khriston, ke sothisi si ke o ikos soo. — Praxees ton Apostolon xvi. 31.

il sangue di Gesù Cristo suo figliuolo, ci purga d'ogni peccato.— Prima Epistola di San Giovanni i. 7.

to ema I-isoo Khristoo too i-ioo avtoo katharizee imas apo pasis amartias.—Proti Epistoli Ioannoo i. 7.

ecco l'agnello di Dio, che toglie il peccato del mondo.—Evangelo di San Giovanni i. 29.

ide o amnes too Theoo, o eron tin amartian too kosmoo. — Evanghelion kata Ioannin i. 29.

Jesus Christ came into the world to save sinners; of whom I am the chief.—1 Timothy i. 15.

How shall we escape if we neglect so great salvation?—Heb. ii. 3.

Whosoever will, let him take the water of life freely.—Revelation xxii. 17.

The Son of man is come to seek and to save that which was lost.—Luke xix. 10.

Whosoever shall call upon the name of the Lord shall be saved.—Romans x. 13.

He that spared not His own Son, but delivered Him up for us all, now shall He not with Him also freely give us all things?—Romans viii. 32.

messīh "īssà dùnyāya ghyùnāh-kerleri khàlāss itmek ichin ghèldi bùnnarin birinjissi bèn im.—1 timutaus i bābb. 10.

bùila "àzīm khàlāssi ìhmāl ìtti-ghimiz tàkdīrda bìz nàssl nèjāt bòlajaghiz. — "ibràniler ikinji bāb. 4.

sū sìyān ghèlsin vè ìssteyān hà-yāt sūindan mèjjānan àlsiu.—yùhannanin vàhissi xxii. 17.

ibn àl-inssān zāyi" òlani àrayub khàlāss itmagha ghèldi dedi.—luka xix. 10.

hèr kìm rābbin ìssmina dù"à ìdcrsa khàlāss bòlajakdir. — ròmalilara x. 13.

kèndi òghlini èssirghmeyub àni bìzim jùmlèmiz ichin tèsslīm èylayān àninila bèrāber hèr shèyi dakhi bìza nàssl īhssān ìtmayājakdir.—ròmalilara viii. 32.

Cristo Gesù è venuto nel mendo, per salvare peccatori, dei quali io sono il primo.—2 Timoteo i. 15.

come scamperemo noi, se trascuriamo una cotante salute?—Ebrei ii. 3.

chi vuele, prenda in dono dell 'acqua della vita.—Apocalisse xxii. 17.

il figliuol dell' uomo è venuto per cercare, e per salvare ciò che era perito.—San Luca xix. 10.

chiunque avrà invocato il nome del Signore sara salvato.—Remani x. 13.

che non ha risparmiato il suo proprio figliuolo, anzi l' ha dato per tutte noi, come non ci donerebbe egli ancora tutte le cese con lui?—Remani viii. 32.

oti Khristos I-isoos ilthen ees ton kosmon amartoloos sese, on protos eemi eghò.—Pres Timetheon i. 15.

pos imees ekfevxometha tilikavtis amelisantes sotirias.—Pros Ebreeos ii. 3.

o thelon lambaneto to ider zeis dorean.—Apokalipsis xxii. 17.

ilthe ghar o i-ios too anthropoo zitise ke sese to apololos. — Lukan xix. 10.

pas ghar os an epikalesite to onoma Kirioo, sothisete.—Pros Romeoos x. 13.

os ghe too idioo i-ioo ook efeesato, all' iper imon panton paredoken avton, pos ookhi ke sin avto ta panta imin kharisete. — Pros Romeoos viii. 32.

STEPHEN AUSTIN AND SONS, PRINTERS, HERTFORD.

14, Henrietta Street, Covent Garden, London; and
20, South Frederick Street, Edinburgh.

WILLIAMS AND NORGATE'S

LIST OF

𝔉𝔯𝔢𝔫𝔠𝔥, 𝔊𝔢𝔯𝔪𝔞𝔫, 𝔍𝔱𝔞𝔩𝔦𝔞𝔫, 𝔏𝔞𝔱𝔦𝔫, 𝔞𝔫𝔡 𝔊𝔯𝔢𝔢𝔨,

AND OTHER

SCHOOL BOOKS AND MAPS.

------•-•-•------

𝔉𝔯𝔢𝔫𝔠𝔥.

Eugène (G.) The Student's Comparative Grammar of the French
Language, with an Historical Sketch of the Formation
of French. For the use of Public Schools. With Exercises. 2nd Improved Edition. Square crown 8vo,
cloth. 5s.
Or Grammar, 3s.; Exercises, 2s. 6d.

"The appearance of a Grammar like this is in itself a sign that great
advance is being made in the teaching of modern as well as of ancient languages. . . . . The rules and observations are all scientifically classified and
explained. . . . . Mr. Eugène's book is one that we can strongly recommend
for use in the higher forms of large schools."—*Educational Times.*

"In itself this is in many ways the most satisfactory Grammar for beginners that we have as yet seen. . . . . The book is likely to be useful to all
who wish either to learn or to teach the French language."—*Athenæum.*

Eugène's French Method. Elementary French Lessons. Easy
Rules and Exercises preparatory to the "Student's Com-
parative French Grammar." By the same Author. 2nd
Edition. Crown 8vo, cloth. 1s. 6d.

"Certainly deserves to rank among the best of our Elementary French
Exercise-books."—*Educational Times.*

"To those who begin to study French, I may recommend, as the best
book of the kind with which I am acquainted, 'Eugène's Elementary Lessons in French.' It is only after having fully mastered this small manual
and Exercise-book that they ought to begin the more systematic study of
French."—*Dr. Breymann, Lecturer of the French Language and Litera-
ture, Owens College, Manchester (Preface to Philological French Grammar).*

Eugène's Comparative French-English Studies, Grammatical and Idiomatic. Being a Second, entirely re-written, Edition of the " French Exercises for Middle and Upper Forms." Cloth.   2s. 6d.

Attwell (H.) Twenty Supplementary French Lessons, with Etymological Vocabularies. Chiefly for the use of Schools where Latin is taught. Crown 8vo, cloth.   2s.

Krueger (H.) Short French Grammar. 4th Edition. 180 pp. 12mo, cloth.   2s.

Eugène (G.) French Irregular Verbs scientifically classified with constant Reference to Latin. Reprinted from his Grammar. 8vo, sewed.   6d.

Menard (Prof. J.) Short Rules and Tables for Conjugating the French Verbs. 8vo, cloth.   1s.

Ahn's French Familiar Dialogues, and French-English Vocabulary for English Schools. 12mo, cloth.   2s.

Brasseur (Prof. Isid.) Grammar of the French Language, comprehending New and complete Rules on the Genders of French Nouns. 20th Edition. 12mo, cloth.   3s. 6d.

———— Key to the French Grammar. 12mo, cloth.   3s.

———— Selection from Chesterfield's and Cowper's Letters, with Notes for translating. 5th Edition. 12mo, cloth.   3s.

———— Key. Partie Française du Choix des Lettres. 12mo, cloth.   3s. 6d.

———— Manuel des Ecoliers. A French Reading Book, preceded by Rules on French Pronunciation. 6th Edition. 12mo.   2s. 6d.

———— Premières Lectures. An easy French Reading Book for Children and Beginners. 18mo, cloth.   1s. 6d.

Roche (A.) Nouvelle Grammaire Française. Nouvelle Edition. 12mo, boards.   1s.

Williams (T. S.) and J. Lafont. French and Commercial Correspondence. A Collection of Modern Mercantile Letters in French and English, with their translation on opposite pages. 2nd Edition. 12mo, cloth.   4s. 6d.
For a German Version of the same Letters, vide p. 4.

Fleury's Histoire de France, racontée à la Jeunesse, edited for the use of English Pupils, with Grammatical Notes, by Auguste Beljame, Bachelier-ès-lettres de l'Université de Paris. 2nd Edition. 12mo, cloth boards.   3s. 6d.

Mandrou (A.) Album Poétique de la Jeunesse. A Collection of French Poetry, selected expressly for English Schools by A. Mandrou, M.A. de l'Academie de Paris, Professor of French in the Clergy Orphan School, St. Peter's Collegiate School, the Crystal Palace, &c. 12mo, cloth. 3s. 6d.

Couronne Enchantée. Contes de Fées. 18mo, cloth. 1s. 6d.

German.

Weisse's Complete Practical Grammar of the German Language, with Exercises on Conversations, Letters, Poems and Treatises, &c. 3rd Edition, very much improved. 12mo, cloth. 6s.

—— New Conversational Exercises in German Composition, with complete Rules and Directions, with full References to his German Grammar. 2nd Edition. 12mo, cloth. 3s. 6d.

Schlutter's German Class Book. A Course of Instruction based on Becker's System, and so arranged as to exhibit the Self-development of the Language, and its Affinities with the English. By Fr. Schlutter, Royal Military Academy, Woolwich. 3rd Edition. 12mo, cloth. 5s.

Möller (A.) A German Reading Book. A Companion to Schlutter's German Class Book. With a complete Vocabulary. 150 pp. 12mo, cloth. 2s.

Wittich's German Grammar. 7th Edition. 12mo, cloth. 6s. 6d.

—— German for Beginners. New Edition. 12mo, cloth. 5s.

—— Key to ditto. 12mo, cloth. 7s.

—— German Tales for Beginners, arranged in Progressive Order. 20th Edition. Crown 8vo, cloth. 6s.

Ravensberg (A. v.) Practical Grammar of the German Language. Conversational Exercises, Dialogues and Idiomatic Expressions. 2 vols. in 1. 12mo, cloth. 5s.

—— Key to the Exercises. Cloth. 2s.

—— Rose's English into German. A Selection of Anecdotes, Stories, Portions of Comedies, &c., with copious Notes for Translation into English. By A. v. Ravensberg. 2nd Edition. 2 Parts in 1. Cloth. 4s. 6d.

—— Key to Rose's English into German. Cloth. 5s.

Ravensberg (A. v.) German Reader, Prose and Poetry, with copious Notes for Beginners. 2nd Edition. Crown 8vo, cloth. 3s.

———— Student's First Year's German Companion. A concise Conversational Method for Beginners. 12mo, cloth. 2s.6d.

Sonnenschein and Stallybrass. German for the English. Part I. First Reading Book. Easy Poems with interlinear Translations, and illustrated by Notes and Tables, chiefly Etymological. 4th Edition. 12mo, cloth. 4s. 6d.

Ahn's German Method by Rose. A New Edition of the genuine Book, with a Supplement consisting of Models of Conjugations, a Table of all Regular Dissonant and Irregular Verbs, Rules on the Prepositions, &c. &c. By A. V. Rose. 2 Courses in 1 vol. Cloth. 3s. 6d.

———— German Method by Rose, &c. First Course. Cloth. 2s.

Apel's Short and Practical German Grammar for Beginners, with copious Examples and Exercises. 2nd Edition. 12mo, cloth. 2s. 6d.

[Black's] Thieme's Complete Grammatical German Dictionary, in which are introduced the Genitives and Plurals and other Irregularities of Substantives, the Comparative Degrees of Adjectives, and the Irregularities of Verbs. Square 8vo, strongly bound. 6s.

Koehler (F.) German-English and English-German Dictionary. 2 vols. 1120 pp., treble columns, royal 8vo, in one vol., half-bound. 9s.

Williams (T. S.) Modern German and English Conversations and Elementary Phrases, the German revised and corrected by A. Kokemueller. 21st enlarged and improved Edition. 12mo, cloth. 3s. 6d.

———— and C. Cruse. German and English Commercial Correspondence. A Collection of Modern Mercantile Letters in German and English, with their Translation on opposite pages. 12mo, cloth. 4s. 6d.

For a French Version of the same Letters, vide p. 2.

Sohl (J.) Forty-eight Lessons in German. A Course comprehending Exercises, Conversations, Composition and Reader, with Vocabularies. 8vo. 3s.

Apel (M.) German Prose Stories for Beginners (including Lessing's Prose Fables), with an interlinear Translation in the natural order of Construction. 12mo, cloth. 2s. 6d.

Apel (M.) German Poetry. A Collection of German Poetry for the use of Schools and Families, containing nearly 300 Pieces selected from the Works of 70 different Authors. Crown 8vo, cloth. 5s.

——— German Prose. A Collection of the best Specimens of German Prose, chiefly from Modern Authors. A Handbook for Schools and Families. 500 pp. Crown 8vo, cloth. 3s.

Andersen (H. C.) Bilderbuch Ohne Bilder. The German Text, with Explanatory Notes, &c., and a complete Vocabulary, for the use of Schools, by Alphons Beck. 12mo, cloth limp. 2s.

Chamisso's Peter Schlemihl. The German Text, with copious Explanatory Notes and a Vocabulary, by M. Förster. Crown 8vo, cloth. 2s.

Goethe's Hermann und Dorothea. With Grammatical and Explanatory Notes, and a complete Vocabulary, by M. Förster. 12mo, cloth. 2s. 6d.

——— Hermann und Dorothea. With Grammatical Notes by A. von Ravensberg. Crown 8vo, cloth. 2s. 6d.

——— Hermann und Dorothea. The German Text, with corresponding English Hexameters on opposite pages. By F. B. Watkins, M.A., Professor of Greek and Latin, Queen's College, Liverpool. Crown 8vo, cloth. 3s.

——— Egmont. The German Text, with Explanatory Notes and a complete Vocabulary, by H. Apel. 12mo, cloth. 2s. 6d.

——— Faust. With copious Notes by Falk Lebahn. 8vo, cloth. 10s. 6d.

Goldschmidt (H. E.) German Poetry. A Selection of the best Modern Poems, with the best English Translations on opposite pages. Crown 8vo, cloth. 5s.

Hauff's Mærohen. A Selection from Hauff's Fairy Tales. The German Text, with a Vocabulary in foot-notes. By A. Hoare, B.A. Crown 8vo, cloth. 3s. 6d.

Nieritz. Die Waise, a German Tale, with numerous Explanatory Notes for Beginners, and a complete Vocabulary, by E. C. Otte. 12mo, cloth. 2s. 6d.

Carové (J. W.) Mæhrchen ohne Ende (The Story without an End). 12mo, cloth. 2s.

Lessing's Minna von Barnhelm. The German Text, with Explanatory Notes for translating into English, and a complete Vocabulary, by J. A. F. Schmidt. 12mo, cloth. 2s. 6d.

Schiller's Song of the Bell. German Text, with English Poetical Translation on the opposite pages, by J. Hermann Merivale, Esq. 12mo, cloth.   1s.

Fouque's Undine, Sintram, Aslauga's Ritter, die beiden Hauptleute. 4 vols in 1. 8vo, cloth.   7s. 6d.

Undine. 1s. 6d.; cloth, 2s.   Aslauga. 1s. 6d.; cloth, 2s.
Sintram. 2s. 6d.; cloth, 3s.   Hauptleute. 1s. 6d.; cloth, 2s.

Latin and Greek.

Thompson (Prof. D'Arcy) Latin Grammar for Elementary Classes. 12mo, cloth.   2s.

Jessopp (Rev. Dr.) Manual of Greek Accidence. New Edition. Crown 8vo.   3s. 6d.

Bryce (Rev. Dr.) The Laws of Greek Accentuation Simplified. 3rd Edition, with the most essential Rules of Quantity. 12mo, sewed.   6d.

Euripides' Medea. The Greek Text, with Introduction and Explanatory Notes for Schools, by J. H. Hogan. 8vo, cloth.   3s. 6d.

——— Ion. Greek Text, with Notes for Beginners, Introduction and Questions for Examination, by the Rev. Charles Badham, D.D. 2nd Edition. 8vo.   3s. 6d.

Æschylus. Agamemnon. Revised Greek Text, with literal line-for-line Translation on opposite pages, by John F. Davies, B.A. 8vo, cloth.   3s.

Platonis Philebus. With Introduction and Notes by Dr. C. Badham. 2nd Edition, considerably augmented. 8vo, cloth.

——— Euthydemus et Laches. With Critical Notes and an Epistola critica to the Senate of the Leyden University, by the Rev. Ch. Badham, D.D. 8vo, cloth.   4s.

——— Symposium, and Letter to the Master of Trinity, "De Platonis Legibus,"—Platonis Convivium, cum Epistola ad Thompsonum edidit Carolus Badham. 8vo, cloth. 4s.

Sophocles. Electra. The Greek Text critically revised, with the aid of MSS. newly collated and explained. By Rev. H. F. M. Blaydes, M.A., formerly Student of Christ Church, Oxford. 8vo, cloth. 6s.

———— Philoctetes. Edited by the same. 8vo, cloth. 6s.

———— Trachiniæ. Edited by the same. 8vo, cloth. 6s.

———— Ajax. Edited by the same. 8vo, cloth. 6s.

Kiepert's New Atlas Antiquus. Maps of the Ancient World, for Schools and Colleges. 6th Edition. With a complete Geographical Index. Folio, boards. 7s. 6d.

———— The Index may be had separately. 1s. 6d.

Italian.

Volpe (Cav. G.) Eton Latin Grammar, for the use of Eton College. Including Exercises and Examples. New Edition. Crown 8vo, cloth. 4s. 6d.

———— Key to the Exercises. 1s.

Rossetti. Exercises for securing Idiomatic Italian by means of Literal Translations from the English, by Maria F. Rossetti. 12mo, cloth. 3s. 6d.

———— Aneddoti Italiani. One Hundred Italian Anecdotes, selected from "Il Compagno del Passeggio." Being also a Key to Rossetti's Exercises. 12mo, cloth. 2s. 6d.

Spanish.

Ollendorff's Method applied to the Spanish Language, by Velasquez and Simonné. 12mo, bound. 6s.

———— Key to ditto. 12mo. 4s.

Velasquez. Larger Spanish Dictionary, composed from the Dictionaries of the Spanish Academy, Terreros and Salva. Spanish-English and English-Spanish. 1279 pp., treble columns. 2 vols. in 1. Impl. 8vo, cloth. 24s.

Velasquez. Spanish and English Dictionary. Abridged from the Author's larger Work. 2 vols. in 1. Crown 8vo, bound. 10*s.* 6*d.*

Kinloch (A.) Compendium of Portuguese Grammar. 12mo, cloth. 4*s.* 6*d.*

𝔇𝔞𝔫𝔦𝔰𝔥—𝔇𝔲𝔱𝔠𝔥.

Bojesen (Mad. Marie) The Danish Speaker. Pronunciation of the Danish Language, Vocabulary, Dialogues and Idioms for the use of Students and Travellers in Denmark and Norway. 12mo, cloth. 4*s.*

Rask (E.) Danish Grammar for Englishmen. With Extracts in Prose and Verse. 2nd Edition. Edited by Repp. 8vo. 5*s.*

Ferrall, Repp, and Rosing. Danish-English and English-Danish Dictionary. New Edition. 2 Parts in 1. Square 8vo. 14*s.*

Williams and Ludolph. Dutch and English Dialogues, and Elementary Phrases. 12mo. 2*s.* 6*d.*

𝔚𝔞𝔩𝔩 𝔐𝔞𝔭𝔰.

Sydow's Wall Maps of Physical Geography for School-rooms, representing the purely physical proportions of the Globe, drawn on a very large scale. An English Edition, the Originals with English Names and Explanations. Mounted on canvas, with rollers:

1. The World. 12 Sheets. Mounted. 10*s.*
2. Europe. 9 Sheets. Mounted. 10*s.*
3. Asia. 9 Sheets. Mounted. 10*s.*
4. Africa. 6 Sheets. 10*s.*
5. America (North and South). 2 Maps, 10 Sheets. Mounted. 10*s.*
6. Australia and Australasia. 6 Sheets. Mounted. 10*s.*

—— Handbook to the Series of Large Physical Maps for School Instruction, edited by J. Tilleard. 8vo. 1*s.*

CPSIA information can be obtained
at www.ICGtesting.com
Printed in the USA
BVHW042205291018
531626BV00015B/148/P

9 781333 904746